A.M.C. FIELD GUIDE

TO

MOUNTAIN FLOWERS

OF

NEW ENGLAND

Appalachian Mountain Club

5 Joy Street, Boston, Mass.

PUBLISHER'S PREFACE TO THE 1977 EDITION.

In the years since the Appalachian Mountain Club first published this book as *Mountain Flowers of New England,* much has happened in and to the mountainous backcountry of this nation's most populous region. Most obvious to anyone who has traversed the New England hills is that over the last decade hiking has undergone a renaissance. What was the eccentric pursuit of a small number of devotees has become in a mere dozen years a respectable leisure for millions of people.

This book is for the hundreds of thousands who hike the New England backcountry. The Appalachian Mountain Club hopes this handy little volume will acquaint many uninitiated backpackers with the wonderful microscopic world at their feet. For the true wilderness experience embraces the wild and the tame, the beautiful and the brutal, the grand and the small. The paradox is this: when you finally begin to sense the true dimensions of the diminutive world of mountain flora, you will have begun to know the real vastness of the seemingly congested New England wilderness.

The *AMC Field Guide to Mountain Flowers of New England* was written by Stuart K. Harris, Jean H. Langenheim, and Frederick L. Steele. Miriam Underhill did the photography. This edition contains a key to common plants found in the fall above treeline on Mount Washington, compiled by Christine Johnson of Trent University, Peterborough, Ontario. Walter S. Graff, Programs Director at AMC Pinkham Notch Camp, assisted in preparing the key for inclusion in the book. To all of these people, the AMC is indebted.

The Appalachian Mountain Club wishes you good hiking and hopes you enjoy your excursion into the exciting world of mountain flowers.

W. Kent Olson

INTRODUCTION

The plants growing on the New England and New York mountains are quite different from the lowland plants of the surrounding countryside. They are of great interest to botanists because of their similarity to plants in the Arctic regions. A strong probability is that these plants had their genesis locally during the Ice Age. As the great ice-sheets advanced southward, the climate became cooler and created conditions in which Arctic plants could grow. Conversely, as the ice retreated to the north, so generally did the plants. Many of them, however, found the high winds, cold, moisture, and frequent cloud-cover that exist in our mountains similar to arctic conditions and have remained with us. Most of these arctic-alpine species, growing in what has been called an "island of vegetation," reach their southern limits for the eastern United States here in our New England mountains.

Botanists were aware of these unusual plants some two hundred years ago. Many of our mountain features on the Presidential Range in the White Mountains are named for early botanist-explorers. Some that come to mind are the Cutler River, Tuckerman Ravine, Huntington Ravine, Oakes Gulf, Boott Spur, and Bigelow Lawn.

Today, not only botanists but mountain walkers find these small but charming flowers most attractive. This book is our answer to the many inquiries we receive concerning them. We have attempted to describe not only the arctic-alpine species but also all the plants that are likely to be found on the mountaintops. Also we have included some which ascend to the alpine areas from the spruce-fir forests below and from the lowlands.

Stuart K. Harris, Professor of Biology at Boston University, has written the main body of the book, VASCULAR PLANTS, and has also drawn the sketches. Starting as a hutman at the Lakes-of-the-Clouds Hut in 1927, he has been associated with the Appalachian Mountain Club for many years. From 1940 to 1949 he wrote a series of articles on the plants of the Presidential Range for *Appalachia*, the magazine of the Appalachian Mountain Club. To this material has been added many species covering other mountain ranges of New Hampshire, Katahdin and other mountains in Maine, the Green Mountains in Vermont, and the Adirondacks. While the alpine areas occur more commonly at elevations between 4000 and 5000 feet we have covered not only the upper slopes of the higher mountains but also the open rocky summits of lower peaks. In fact, we have tried to cover any terrain that has an alpine aspect.

Jean H. Langenheim, Research Fellow in Biology at Harvard, has written the section on LICHENS AND MOSSES. This section was not intended to cover these plants completely, but rather to serve as a brief introduction. For those whose appetite has been whetted by this introduction a bibliography of suggested readings has been added. Dr. Langenheim has done research on mountain plants in Alaska, the Rocky Mountains, the Sierra Nevada, and in Colombia.

Frederic L. Steele, teacher of science at St. Mary's-in-the-Mountains School in Littleton, New Hampshire, has helped in many ways. Specifically, he has searched out the species which occur outside the Presidential Range.

Miriam Underhill was chairman of the committee which was responsible for the preparation of this book. Mrs. Underhill, formerly editor of *Appalachia*, took the original color photographs from which the color plates were made. Although she will protest that it was a labor of love we should be remiss were we not to recognize her untiring efforts on behalf of this production.

The above four members of the Club have prepared what we think is an excellent book, which the Club is happy to offer to its members and to the public.

ACKNOWLEDGMENTS

We extend our grateful thanks to the following people who have greatly assisted us. In connection with Dr. Langenheim's section on LICHENS AND MOSSES, to Dr. W. A. Weber, University of Colorado, for checking determinations of the lichens; to Dr. L. C. Bliss, University of Illinois, for his discussions concerning the ecology of lichens on Mt. Washington; and to Dr. I. M. Lamb, Harvard University, for his many helpful conversations as well as criticism of the manuscript.

In connection with the distribution of plants we further acknowledge our thanks to the late Professor A. S. Pease; Dr. A. E. Brower of the State of Maine Forest Service; Dr. Hubert Vogelmann, Department of Botany, University of Vermont; Mr. Leopold Charette, Pringle Herbarium, University of Vermont; Dr. Albion R. Hodgdon, Department of Botany, University of New Hampshire; Mr. A. W. Bromley, New York State Conservation Department.

To the Swiss Alpine Club who, unknown to themselves, have provided us, through their book, *Unsere Alpenflora*, with many excellent ideas.

Appalachian Mountain Club

LICHENS AND MOSSES

In alpine areas the world over, as well as in arctic ones, lichens and mosses grow amid the colorful herbs, dwarfed shrubs, and tufts of grasses and sedges. In the alpine areas in the Presidential Range, in particular, lichens reach greater abundance and play a more important role in the development of the vegetation than in most other mountainous areas in the United States. It is because of their conspicuous abundance and their significance in the vegetation that we introduce the lichens to those interested in the alpine plants of the New England mountains. The mosses, although they are of lesser importance, are also fascinating when one's eyes are opened to their presence. In both cases no attempt has been made to discuss other than a few of the most conspicuous species, especially those that can be seen on Mt. Washington.

Because the lichen has such a distinctive plant body, pointing out a few facts about its structure may be helpful in identifying these plants. The plant body or *thallus* is a composite structure, made up of microscopic strands (*hyphae*) of a fungus and usually a single-celled alga. This thallus, resulting from the union of the fungus and alga, is entirely different from that formed by either component when grown alone. The fungal hyphae for the most part determine the shape, appearance and consistency of the lichen thallus. The lichen fungi contain no chlorophyll and depend upon the photosynthetic activity of the algae for their food. In fact, it has even been said that the lichen in reality is a fungus that imitates a green plant by using another plant to take care of its food manufacture. The algal cells, however, gain by being surrounded by the fungal hyphae in protection against dessication and strong sunlight as well as in a supply of inorganic substances. Actually the fungus is a controlled parasite of the alga. Because both organisms appear to derive mutual benefit from this relationship, however, it is called symbiosis or consortism. As a result of this arrangement, lichens have a truly remarkable resistance to drought and dessication, which enables them to occupy some of the most severe and forbidding habitats on earth. This is one of the reasons that we see them so commonly in high mountain environments, where no other plants are sufficiently hardy to exist. Also, because an individual colony can attain a very old age, lichens are sometimes described as "time stains." Certain lichens have been estimated to be more than two thousand years old, which is more ancient than some of the oldest redwood trees. Because they grow slowly and the rate of growth can easily be measured, lichens provide evidence of the age of such geological phenomena as glacial moraines and lava flows.

Lichens are commonly divided into three groups based upon their growth forms. Those which form a crust which is firmly attached to the soil, rock, or bark are called *crustose*. The *foliose* types form leafy structures which are less firmly attached to their substratum than the crustose forms. The third type, known as *fruticose*, grows directly from its base in elongated stalks, which are either upright or pendulous.

The reproductive sacs which liberate spores are borne in various types of fruiting bodies. Some are globular or lumpy, whereas others are saucer-shaped. The spores come only from the fungal component. If they are to produce another lichen, they must come into contact with a free-living alga of the appropriate species. Unfortunately these species appear to be rare outside the lichens. Thus there is serious question as to whether the lichen depends to any extent upon this type of reproduction. It certainly appears that the most common type of reproduction is one which circumvents this complex problem of the fungal spore finding the right kind of algal cell. A fragment broken from any part, provided it contains algal cells and drops into a favorable habitat, may develop into another complete lichen. This breakage accounts for much of the dissemination of lichens. Moreover, many lichens have accessory structures for vegetative propagation known as *isidia* and *soredia*. The isidia are either granules or coral-like growths, which function as a part of the lichen until they are broken off. These structures are actually lichens in miniature. Soredia are less well organized structures than the isidia. They consist of grains containing algal cells enclosed in fungal threads, which develop on the surface of the lichen. They usually appear as pale gray, green or yellow dust. occurring on a special part of the lichen or all over it, and dusted thinly or collected in clusters.

In identifying lichens, the nature of the growth form is important in separating genera. Fruiting bodies and spores are particularly important in determining species of the crustose types; isidia and soredia assume this role among the foliose and fruticose forms. Lichens secrete a number of unique organic compounds, called lichen acids, which are deposited in definite layers of tissue. The present trend in lichen taxonomy is to attempt to identify these lichen acids by color tests, crystal tests and chromatography. Many lichens with the same morphological form show different chemical strains. This appears to indicate to many botanists that biochemical evolution either precedes that shown in the form of the organism or maybe takes place independently.

Much beauty in our natural landscape would be lost without mosses because of the color, bright greens or rusty reds, which they add. This is especially true in alpine areas where, except for a short period of showy flowering, the aspect may be somber. They also play a significant role in moisture conservation. In some types of vegetation, such as sedge meadows, mosses provide seed beds as well as a subsequent favorable habitat for herbaceous and shrubby plants. They themselves seem quite independent of variation in climate. In damp weather they grow with amazing rapidity, and in dry or frozen periods they suspend growth. Although there is a variety of mosses to be discovered in the alpine areas in the New England mountains, we are introducing only two groups, the peat mosses (*Sphagnum*) and the hair-cap mosses (*Polytrichum*).

Mosses (particularly *Polytrichum*) and lichens (especially members of the fruticose genera *Cetraria* and *Cladonia*) are very conspicuous in meadows dominated by Bigelow sedge. Although the mosses become less significant, the lichens are still extremely abundant in plant communities containing a mixture of sedges and dwarf shrub heaths such as mountain cranberry, alpine bilberry and diapensia. *Cetraria* and *Cladonia* are also important elements in the three-forked rush—dwarf heath community. These lichens, as well as many other types, occur in most other communities; however, they are less prominent. The occurrence in such abundance of many of these lichens and mosses on Mt. Washington, in particular, has been attributed largely to the exceptional weather conditions. The combination of exceedingly high winds, cloud cover, frequent fog, high precipitation and cool summer temperatures results in a climate similar to that present today in northern Canada and Alaska. It has even been suggested by some botanists working on this flora that the luxuriance of lichens and mosses on Mt. Washington and north through Katahdin, Mt. Albert, and the Arctic reflects high atmospheric moisture and frequent fog.

CRUSTOSE LICHENS

Map Lichen *Rhizocarpon geographicum* (L.) DC. The map lichen forms patches of a thin yellow or greenish crust, which is usually dispersed upon a conspicuously black basal layer. This patchwork of yellow and black covers indefinitely large areas, prominently coloring the higher rocks. "Map lichen" is a graphic and appropriate name, because of the island-like divisions of the patches when they are dry. Fruits are plentiful, disk-shaped or angular, up to $\frac{3}{100}$ of an inch in diameter, black with a black rim, and occurring tightly appressed on the crust. Map lichen is found on exposed rocks at high elevations throughout the United States and is particularly abundant above timberline. Pl. 3, 3 shows the map-like patches of yellow crust on the black under layer, which is found so frequently on the so-called bare rocks.

Stud Lichen   *Ochrolechia frigida* (Sw.) Lynge. The stud lichen consists of a thick silver-gray or whitish crust, which is generally cracked into patches when dry. It forms nearly circular units; the central parts are often warty or covered with coral-like prongs. In the Far North the crust grows rampant over moss and along the ground. The fruits are bowl- to saucer-shaped, about $\frac{1}{5}$ inch in diameter, flesh-colored to brick-red with a gray outer rim. It is commonly distributed throughout arctic tundra areas and some alpine areas. The patchy nature of the crust and the conspicuous fruits are well illustrated in Pl. 3, 1.

FOLIOSE LICHENS

Ring Lichen   *Parmelia centrifuga* (L.) Ach. This lichen occurs on rocks, forming flat rosettes, the branches of which are a little less than $\frac{1}{300}$ inch wide. The branches radiate from a center which deteriorates with age, leaving an irregular ring as much as 4 inches across. This effect leads to the name "ring lichen." The upper portion of the thallus is yellowish, but the lower is straw-colored or whitish. New growth often covers the old in shingle fashion, forming a characteristic pattern. Saucer-shaped fruits, as much as $\frac{1}{3}$ inch in diameter, are chestnut-brown with a pale rim. The ring lichen occurs on alpine and subalpine rocks in the Arctic, in the White Mountains, in Newfoundland, and as far west as the shores of Lake Superior. *Parmelia centrifuga* could be confused with two other members of this genus here. *Parmelia incurva* (Pers.) E. Fries is often found in association with *P. centrifuga* and looks very much like it, being distinguished primarily by the presence of globular masses of yellowish soredia. *Parmelia conspersa* (Ehrh.) Ach. is also similar to the ring lichen. It is one of the most plentiful of this genus, occurring frequently in the North. It does not grow commonly above timberline, however, and is smaller than *P. centrifuga*. In Pl. 1, 4 the branching system of the rosette is illustrated, although the ring effect is not apparent in this example.

Rock Tripe   *Umbilicaria hyperborea* Ach. Rock tripe forms leathery, irregularly circular sheets which are attached to the rocks by a strong central umbilicus. These sheets are usually $1\frac{1}{2}$ inches across, much crumpled and often complicated by overlapping lobes. The upper surface is blackish to chocolate brown with densely crowded blisters or warts, and sometimes numerous perforations occur toward the irregular margins. The name is derived from the fact that it is considered edible, and possibly from its textural similarity to tripe. The disk-shaped or angular fruiting bodies are common. Although they occur up to $\frac{1}{20}$ inch across, they are usually smaller. This lichen grows in the White Mountains, primarily above timberline, as well as in the western mountains. There are several species of *Umbilicaria* that occupy alpine environments, usually growing on exposed cliffs and boulders. In this area it is difficult to distinguish morphologically *U. hyperborea* from *U. proboscidea* (L.) Schrad. and *U. arctica* (Ach.) Nyl., and the three are often seen growing intermingled. Pl. 3, 2 shows the typical general appearance of the thallus of these rock tripes. The map lichen is seen in the background and immediate foreground.

FRUTICOSE LICHENS

Reindeer Lichen *Cladonia rangiferina* (L.) Web. The Cladonias are the most familiar of all lichens, and probably have been collected more frequently than any other genus. There are numerous species which are often difficult to distinguish. Chemical tests are important in the Cladonias and must be used to identify some species. Many species of *Cladonia* may be found in the Presidential Range, but because of difficulties in determination, we are introducing only three very characteristic and abundant species which are relatively easy to differentiate. The reindeer lichen, so commonly and erroneously called "reindeer moss," is made up of tufts, sometimes 10 inches or more across, in which the constituent stalks tend to be tangled. The stalks, very slender and about 2 inches high, may fork and branch into whorls. Most of the tops of the stalks turn downward, subdividing into several fine, drooping, finger-like structures. Brown fruits, commonly $\frac{3}{100}$ inch in diameter, sometimes occur on the tips. Whitish soredia occasionally form along the older stalks. The reindeer lichen is found on soil and on ledges of rock in exposed places throughout the northern United States and is fairly common high in the mountains. It is abundant throughout the arctic tundra regions, producing fodder for reindeer, caribou and other animals. During famines Scandinavians have been known to grind it and mix it with flour to make bread. Pl. 1, 2 shows the characteristic drooping tips of the stalks. This lichen grows upright, however, and as a whole is not pendulous as might be interpreted from this picture.

Alpine Reindeer Lichen   *Cladonia alpestris* (L.) Rabh. Tufts of young plants of this lichen show an attachment to the ground, but as the plant grows its lower parts decay, more or less detaching the tufts. The tufts consist of compound domes about an inch across. The branching system is basically different from that of *C. rangiferina*. It is much denser and each branchlet grows stiffly outward on a radius of the dome, then dividing almost at right angles, so that its several spreading divisions follow the circumference of the dome. Other reindeer lichens have branches typically curving outward and ending in tips which droop. Also *C. rangiferina* is pure gray to white whereas *C. alpestris* is yellowish in color. The alpine reindeer moss is found throughout the United States, mostly on mountain tops. Characteristic tufts of this lichen are well illustrated in Pl. 1, 3.

British Soldiers   *Cladonia cristatella* Tuck. The stalks of British Soldiers are rod-shaped or variously branched and slightly less than 1 inch high. They arise from a base of "sod flakes" which are greenish-gray when wet or straw-colored when dry. Fruits on the tips of the branches are globular or lumpy, up to $\frac{1}{10}$ inch in diameter. They are usually scarlet, accounting for the name "British Soldiers." It is found on the ground, on tree bark, dead wood, fences, and sometimes on rock throughout the United States. However, *C. coccifera* has red fruits which sit on the rim of the cup rather than a red globular fruiting structure. In Pl. 1, 1 the red fruits of British Soldiers are shown. In the immediate foreground is a gray-green cup fruiting structure of another species of *Cladonia*.

Iceland Lichen   *Cetraria islandica* (L.) Ach. Iceland lichen forms tufts and tangled masses of strap-shaped and forking stalks. The tufts are usually about 2 inches high but may be twice as large. The plant appears quite different in form when it is wet and when it is dry. When wet the stalks are olive green and smooth, with tiny soft spines at the outer margins. When dry the stalks fold inward, forming a central trough edged with dry, stiff spines. The fruits, which are dark brown and borne along margins of enlarged tips of the stalk, are relatively uncommon. They are oval, up to $\frac{1}{2}$ inch across, and the rim is ragged or spiny. Iceland lichen is one of the most important lichens, long used in northern countries both for fodder and for medicinal purposes. In the arctic tundra, large areas may be covered with it, often together with reindeer lichen. It is also plentiful along parts of the New England coast to the Carolinas, and westward to the Pacific coast. It is, however, most common in alpine areas. The Iceland lichen is easily recognized and should not be mistaken for any other lichen except its variety

Delisaei (sometimes considered a separate species *C. hiascens* (Fr.) Th. Fr.). This variety has denser tufts, with wide stalks and narrower tips, and is paler in color than the typical form. Well developed fruiting bodies of Iceland lichen are illustrated in Pl. 2, 1. The dry brown thallus is shown mixed with the pale-yellow snow lichen in Pl. 2, 2.

Snow Lichen   *Cetraria nivalis* (L.) Ach. The tufts of spreading, papery stalks are often 4 inches or more across and $1\frac{1}{2}$ inches high. The stalks branch into broad lobes with finely divided, crinkled tips. The upper surface is pale yellow, covered with a net-like pattern of prominent raised ribs with pits in between. The pale, yellowish-brown fruits are rare. They occur on the margins, and can reach up to $\frac{1}{5}$ inch in diameter. This lichen occurs on soil in the high mountains of northern New England and in the Rocky Mountains. It could hardly be confused with any other lichen, except the similarly colored *C. cucullata* which grows with it. *Cetraria cucullata* (Bell) Ach., or curled lichen, has a quite different branching system. The stalks are rolled into a tube, and the margins splay out at the forks and tips, leaving funnel-shaped openings into the rolled stalk. The crinkled-tipped, pale-yellow thallus of the snow lichen is illustrated in Pl. 2, 2, interspersed with the brown thallus of the Iceland lichen.

Worm Lichen   *Thamnolia vermicularis* (Sw.) Schaer. The stalks are hollow and fragile, simple or slightly divided into horn-shaped branches. They grow to about 3 inches long, often distended in the middle to $\frac{1}{5}$ inch thick, tapering to a narrow base and to a pointed tip. The surface is generally chalky-white, although tending to be gray at the base. The tubular form of the stalk gives it the general appearance of a worm, and hence the name. There are soredia, but fruits are unknown. This lichen is found on tufts of moss or on the ground in the White Mountains and the Adirondacks, as well as in the Rocky Mountains. It is sufficiently unique not to be confused with the reindeer lichens, although it could be mistaken for weather-bleached twigs. Pl. 3, 4 shows the worm-like characteristics of this lichen.

Mane Lichen   *Alectoria ochroleuca* (Hoffm.) Mass. The loosely, arachnoidly-filled, upright stalks of this lichen are somewhat similar to the reindeer lichen. The stalks are sometimes $\frac{1}{10}$ inch thick, forking into an intertangled tuft often more than 3 inches high. They are straw-colored, smooth or slightly wrinkled, and pitted or speckled. The hair-like tips may blacken, making a sharp contrast with the pale stalks and branches. The mane lichen can be distinguished from the reindeer lichen by its hair-like tips and its yellowish color. The fruits, which are not common, occur on the sides of the branches or sometimes near the tips. They are disk-shaped, up to $\frac{1}{3}$ inch in diameter, dark brown with a smooth straw-colored rim. The mane lichen is found on the ground, on rocks and on trees at high altitudes in New England, also in California, and northward. Pl. 3, 5 shows the characteristic hair-like tips which give the appearance of a mane.

MOSSES

Peat Moss *Sphagnum* spp. This genus contains a great many species, found primarily in swamps, bogs and along the margins of ponds and streams. There are several species occurring within our area, but because of the difficulty in distinguishing the species, we shall not attempt to separate them. One species does tend to have a reddish color and patches of it may be seen from great distances; the more common situation is the yellowish-green appearance. In economic value the peat mosses are the most important of the mosses and lichens. The peat of commerce is obtained from the firm, compressed mass of old portions of the plant found in the bottoms of bogs. This mass, cut into bricks and then dried, is used for fuel especially in Scotland and Ireland. Sphagnum also is used for packing material. Gardeners and florists utilize it for packing vegetables and plants, because the peculiar structure of the leaves enables it to absorb and hold moisture like a sponge. The typical form of the *Sphagnum* branches is seen in Pl. 2, 3, although the color is generally paler or more yellowish than that shown in this photograph. Pl. 2, 4 gives an idea of the mass of red color produced by some peat mosses.

Hair-cap Moss *Polytrichum juniperinum* Hedw. var. *alpestre* Bry. Eur. There are over one hundred species included within the hair-cap mosses. They receive their name from the very hairy cap (calyptra) covering the capsule. Some of these species are among our most common mosses, found on soil chiefly in cooler regions. The hair-cap mosses were used in European countries for small brooms and for filling beds. It is said that Linnaeus often slept on such beds. In the alpine areas on Mt. Washington, one of the most important mosses is a variety of *Polytrichum juniperinum*, which appears in great abundance in the sedge meadows. This species ranges from Greenland to Alaska, south to New Jersey, Ohio westward to Wyoming, Colorado, Utah and California. The dwarfed variety occurring above timberline has received the name *alpestre*. Both male and female plants occur together. The leaves have a prominent blue-green cast. This variety might possibly be confused with *P. piliferum* which occurs relatively frequently here. *Polytri-*

8

chum piliferum Hedw. is the smallest hairy-cap moss. The leaves are rather dark green, crowded at the end of the stem. They terminate in a long whitish hair-like tip which gives the plant a hoary appearance. This is a good character to help distinguish *P. piliferum* from *P. juniperinum*. The plants fruit abundantly and are conspicuous in the spring with red fruit stalks and pale yellow hoods. The male plants are often numerous, but do not occur with the female plants as in the *Polytrichum juniperinum*. When the leaves are moist and expanded, the bright red bracts of the rosettes of the male fruiting structures look like tiny flowers. Another possible source of confusion could occur with *Pogonatum alpinum* (Hedw.) Rohl. which is present here. Some authors put *Pogonatum* with *Polytrichum*, but others distinguish *Pogonatum* by cylindric capsules. Pl. 3, 6 shows the capsules of *Polytrichum juniperinum* var. *alpestre*, although the subtle distinction from *Pogonatum alpinum* is not apparent.

JEAN H. LANGENHEIM

ADDITIONAL READING

The following references are suggested for those who might like to learn more about the nature of lichens and mosses, and how to identify species other than those presented in this discussion.

1. Conard, H. S., *How to Know the Mosses*, 2nd edition, 1944. Wm. C. Brown Co., Dubuque, Iowa. Pictured keys for determining many of the North American mosses, with suggestions and aids for their study.
2. Fink, Bruce, *The Lichen Flora of the United States*, 1935. University of Michigan Press, Ann Arbor. A standard work on lichens. Keys to the family and genus are helpful, but difficult to use for species.
3. Grout, A. J., *Mosses with a Hand-Lens*, 3rd edition, 1924. Published by the author, Staten Island, New York. Simple keys to mosses of New England and the Middle Atlantic states, as well as a good discussion of the morphological structures.
4. Hale, M. E., Jr., *Lichen Handbook*, 1961. Smithsonian Institution, Washington, D. C. A guide to the lichens of eastern North America, including very readable general information about lichens.
5. Lamb, I. M., "The Remarkable Lichens," 1958. *Natural History*, vol. 67, pp. 86–93. An excellent popular account of many interesting aspects of lichens.
6. Nearing, G. G., *The Lichen Book*, 1947. Published by the author, Ridgewood, N. J. A handbook of lichens of the northeastern United States.

VASCULAR PLANTS

As one climbs our higher mountains and reaches an elevation of somewhat more than 4000 feet the character of the forest changes. Most of the species seen at lower elevations drop out leaving the balsam fir, black spruce, and paper birch as the only common ones. The individual trees become shorter than those found lower down and many of them are gnarled and misshapen. This is the krummholz or scrub forest. As one ascends farther the krummholz becomes lower and lower until one emerges on the open alpine area. The plants growing on the forest floor, the trees of the krummholz, and the plants of the alpine areas are an interesting group.

The flowering season in this high region begins in May. By mid-June or soon after, the heaths reach their peak of bloom and produce the most spectacular display of the entire season. By early July most of them are through flowering but they are replaced by a steady series of other plants in flower which continues until the killing frosts of late August or early September. A trip to the alpine region late in the season is well worth while to see the display of autumn foliage made by the dwarf birches and some of the heaths. At this time one can often find scattered blossoms of the lapland rosebay and some of the other heaths.

On the Presidential Range in the White Mountains the best base to use in searching for the mountain plants is the Lakes-of-the-Clouds Hut, since from there a majority of them can be found within easy walking distance. The variety about the Madison Huts is much more limited, but many plants can be seen between the Lakes and Madison. As a general rule the botanizing is better on the eastern side of the Range, the choice spots being the area about the Lakes of the Clouds, the Alpine Garden, the Cow Pasture on the Carriage Road, and the vicinity of the Gulf Tank on the Cog Railroad. The headwalls of Oakes Gulf, Tuckerman Ravine, and the Great Gulf should also be explored since a number of plants can be seen along the rills which do not occur on the exposed alpine slopes. Outside the Presidential Range, other bare mountains, such as those of the Franconia Range, the Baldfaces, Guyot, Bondcliff, Cannon Cliffs above the Old Man, present a good showing of alpine plants as do, to a somewhat lesser extent, the more southern peaks like Moosilauke, Chocorua, Cardigan.

In Maine the Katahdin region is outstanding, both the extensive tableland and the walls and gullies running down from it to the basins below. The spectacular display here of arctic-alpine plants includes some species not found farther south. The bare summits of Bigelow, Abraham, Moxie Bald and others are well worth a visit.

Vermont, too, particularly Mt. Mansfield, but also Camel's Hump and other smaller peaks, has a share of alpine plants.

In the Adirondacks, the most extensive alpine area occurs on Mt. Marcy, although some other smaller peaks with open summits present specimens of these plants. In any mountain region, look for treeless areas, preferably damp, and bear in mind that many choice species grow where the winter snow lies deep.

While you can look at and photograph the alpine plants to your heart's content the United States Forest Service prohibits the picking or removal of any flowers or plants, from any part of a national forest, without a written permit. Much the same regulations apply to national parks, state parks or other public reservations. In addition, Vermont has laws concerning the removal of certain plants from private land. These are not unreasonable restrictions since the flora is more than adequately represented by collections made over the past 150 years and on deposit in the herbaria of scientific institutions all over the world. Moreover, while some of the species would make very beautiful rock garden plants their soil and climate requirements are impossible to duplicate at low elevations and when attempts are made to grow them at home they invariably die in a short time.

Starting to learn plants above timberline has the same advantage as beginning to learn birds in the winter: only a limited number of species are involved. Of the two hundred and thirty-odd species included in this book, fewer than one hundred and fifty are likely to be found in any single mountain area while in any lowland township one may have to cope with a thousand or more species of flowering plants. Once one has mastered the plants found above the trees one should be able to recognize related species in the lowlands, thus making their identification much easier.

If you are a beginner, I strongly advise using the scientific names from the start, since it is really much the simplest thing to do and the names are certainly no more formidable than those in the lineup of the average football team. Common names have a number of disadvantages. In the first place more than half the species here treated have no true common names, the names here given being in most cases a translation of the scientific name and never used. Many of the other plants have from two to a dozen common names

11

all being used. Learning *Lycopodium clavatum* is much easier than learning that common clubmoss, running clubmoss, staghorn moss, staghorn evergreen, buckhorn, coral evergreen, wolf's-claws, and pussy-toes are all common names of this species. Furthermore the name *Lycopodium* is applied to all clubmosses, a relationship hidden by such common names as groundpine, groundfir, groundcedar, and heath-cypress applied to four species of clubmosses.

As a help in identification a key to the plant families is given as well as keys to the species within families. In the keys I have attempted to keep the terminology as simple as possible. Each step in the key offers a pair of choices; pick the choice which applies to the plant being identified. At the end of the statement is either a number to indicate the next pair of choices to consider or the name of the family or species to which the plant belongs. Suppose you have a violet. Step one in the key gives the following choices:

1. Leaves all basal . . . . 2.
1. Stem leafy; flowers violet . . . . (5) *Viola adunca*

In your specimen the leaves are all basal so you proceed to step 2.

2. Flowers violet or lilac . . . . 3.
2. Flowers blue or white . . . . 4.

The flowers are white so continue to step 4 in the key.

4. Flowers blue . . . . (1) *Viola cucullata*
4. Flowers white . . . . (4) *Viola pallens*

Your specimen is apparently *V. pallens*. This can be verified by reading the description of that species and checking the specimen with the line drawing in the text and the color photograph on Plate 19. The number in parentheses indicates the number of this species within the family.

The descriptions of species have been kept as simple as possible. A common name has been assigned to each species; if the species has additional common names, these are listed at the end of the description. Every species, save one which was apparently extinct long before it was described, is illustrated by either a color plate or a line drawing, or by both. The scale which appears on many of the line drawings represents one inch and applies to the drawing of the entire plant; the scale of the enlarged details is not usually indicated. If a scale is indicated once on a page containing several drawings, it applies to the entire page.

The following figures demonstrate the meaning of various terms used in the keys and in the descriptions of species.

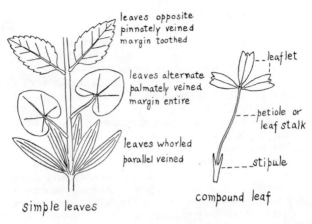

leaves opposite
pinnately veined
margin toothed

leaves alternate
palmately veined
margin entire

leaves whorled
parallel veined

simple leaves

leaflet

petiole or
leaf stalk

stipule

compound leaf

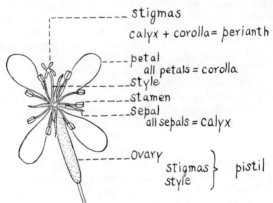

stigmas

calyx + corolla = perianth

petal
all petals = corolla
style
stamen
sepal
all sepals = calyx

ovary

stigmas }
style } pistil

KEY TO THE FAMILIES

1. Aquatic plants growing in or on the water . . . . 2.
1. Terrestrial plants without floating leaves . . . . 4.
    2. Totally submerged plants consisting of a stemless tuft of
       quill-like leaves growing on the bottom

                    Isoëtaceae *Isoëtes muricata* p. 21.
    2. Stemmed plants, floating leaves present or absent . . . 3.
3. Large plants with mature leaves floating and conspicuous
   floating yellow flowers

            Nymphaeaceae *Nuphar variegatum* p. 86.
3. Small inconspicuous plants with mostly submerged leaves

13

and tiny flowers and fruits in leaf axils

Callitrichaceae *Callitriche anceps* p. 100.

4. Plants without flowers; producing spores, not seeds

PTERIDOPHYTA 5.

4. Plants with flowers; producing seeds

SPERMATOPHYTA 8.

5. Sporangia borne on the backs of fronds or portions of fronds . . . . 7.

5. Sporangia borne in the axils of needle-like leaves, or in terminal spikes or cones . . . . 6.

6. Leaves reduced to small scales; vegetative plants plume-like with whorls of green branches at intervals on the stem; sporangia borne in a cone at summit of fertile stem Equisetaceae *Equisetum arvense* p. 18.

6. Leaves numerous on stems and branches, needle-like or scale-like but not greatly reduced Lycopodiaceae p. 18.

7. Sporangia borne on the modified central portion of the frond Osmundaceae *Osmunda Claytoniana* p. 21.

7. Sporangia borne on the backs of leaf-like fronds

Polypodiaceae p. 22.

8. Ovules and seeds borne naked on the faces of scales; fruit in woody or berry-like cones; trees or shrubs with needle-like leaves GYMNOSPERMAE Pinaceae p. 26.

8. Ovules and seeds in a closed ovary ANGIOSPERMAE 9.

9. Floral parts usually in threes; stems not woody; leaves with the principal veins usually parallel

MONOCOTYLEDONEAE 10.

9. Floral parts not in threes; stems woody or herbaceous; leaves usually feather-veined DICOTYLEDONEAE . . 14.

10. Perianth none or reduced to bristles or scales . . . . . 11.

10. Perianth evident, often petal-like or made up of petals and sepals . . . . 12.

11. Stems round or flat, hollow; leaves two-ranked, the sheaths split; anthers of stamens attached at middle Gramineae p. 29.

11. Stems often triangular; leaves three-ranked, the sheaths not split; anthers of stamens attached at base Cyperaceae p. 45.

12. Plants somewhat grass-like; perianth divisions not showy, greenish or brownish Juncaceae p. 62.

12. Plants not grass-like; perianth divisions usually petal-like and showy . . . . 13.

13. Flowers regular; stamens more than three; ovary superior

Liliaceae p. 66.

13. Flowers not regular; stamen one; ovary inferior

Orchidaceae p. 70.

30. Sepals two; distinct

> > > Portulacaceae *Claytonia caroliniana* p. 82.

30. Sepals four or five   Caryophyllaceae p. 83.
31. Flowers regular; leaves not heart-shaped . . . . . . 32.
31. Flowers irregular; leaves heart-shaped   Violaceae p. 104.
  32. Leaves basal, covered with sticky glands

> > > Droseraceae *Drosera rotundifolia* p. 89.

  32. Leaves not as above . . . . 33.
33. Herbs; leaves mostly basal   Saxifragaceae p. 90.
33. Leaves not mostly basal . . . . 34.
  34. Leaves distinctly lobed . . . . 35.
  34. Leaves not distinctly lobed . . . . 36.
35. Erect shrubs with many leaves   Saxifragaceae   *Ribes* p. 92.
35. Creeping herb; erect branches with one to three leaves

> > > Rosaceae *Rubus Chamaemorus* p. 98.

  36. Leaves prominently many-toothed   Rosaceae p. 93.
  36. Leaves entire or with a few obscure teeth

> > > Aquifoliaceae *Nemopanthus mucronatus* p. 102.

37. Leaves not in whorls . . . . 38.
37. Leaves whorled   Cornaceae *Cornus canadensis* p. 111.
  38. Stamens six, two shorter than the other four; seeds with-
    out hairs; leaves alternate or basal   Cruciferae p. 88.
  38. Stamens eight, all of the same length; seeds with a tuft
    of hairs on summit; some of leaves opposite

> > > Onagraceae p. 106.

39. Leaves usually with three leaflets . . . . 40.
39. Leaves with five or more leaflets . . . . 43.
  40. Coarse tall herbs with maple-like leaves; flowers numer-
    ous, borne in umbels

> > > Umbelliferae *Heracleum maximum* p. 110.

  40. Lower and slenderer plants, herbs or shrubs; leaves not
    maple-like; flowers fewer, not borne in umbels . . . . 41.
41. Leaves evergreen; the slender rootstocks bright yellow

> > > Ranunculaceae *Coptis groenlandica* p. 86.

41. Leaves not evergreen; rootstocks not bright yellow . . . 42.
  42. Leaflets entire; soft herbs with a watery juice which is
    acid to taste   Oxalidaceae *Oxalis montana* p. 100.
  42. Leaflets toothed; firmer plants without a watery juice

> > > Rosaceae p. 93.

43. Flowers few, scattered   Rosaceae p. 93.
43. Flowers numerous, in dense inflorescences . . . . . . 44.
  44. Shrubs; leaflets arranged on either side of the main axis

> > > Rosaceae p. 93.

  44. Herbs; leaves distinctly three or more parted . . . . 45.

EQUISETACEAE (Horsetail Family)

The horsetails are a small group of plants which are holdovers from the Coal Age. The stems are usually hollow and jointed; the leaves are reduced to scales arranged in rings about each joint. The plants produce spores rather than seeds; the sporangia are borne

17

in cone-like strobili at the tops of the stems. The strobilus is made up of a considerable number of stalked and somewhat umbrella-shaped sporophylls, each of which bears six or seven sporangia. Only one species is likely to be encountered near the summits of our mountains.

Field Horsetail   *Equisetum arvense* L. In this species both vegetative and fertile stems are produced. The green vegetative stems bear whorls of slender branches and are common throughout the growing season. The brown fertile stems are unbranched and bear a strobilus at the summit; fertile stems appear early in the growing season and soon disintegrate. The species is circumboreal in its distribution. While in no sense an alpine, it has been collected on the summit ridge of Mt. Mansfield and might occasionally be found in other similar habitats. (Common horsetail, meadow pine, devil's-guts.) Fertile and vegetative stems are shown on p. 23, a.

Lycopodiaceae (Clubmoss Family)

The clubmosses are another group which have persisted since very ancient times. Many of them are somewhat moss-like in appearance. They consist of an elongate stem which creeps along the surface of the ground, or just beneath the surface, and sends up erect stems covered with narrow or scale-like leaves. Reproduction is by means of spores; the sporangia are borne either in the axils of the upper leaves or in distinct strobili.

1. Sporangia borne in definite spikes or cones   . . . . 3.
1. Sporangia borne in axils of unmodified leaves   . . . . . . 2.
   2. Leaves uniform in length, broadest at base
                  (1) **Fir Clubmoss**   *Lycopodium Selago*
   2. Leaves in alternating bands of longer and shorter length, broadest above the middle
            (2) **Shining Clubmoss**   *Lycopodium lucidulum*
3. Leaves in eight to ten rows on sterile branches   . . . . . . 4.
3. Leaves in four to five rows on sterile branches   . . . . . . 6.
   4. Ascending branches simple or few-forked, not tree-like . . 5.
   4. Ascending branches freely forking, tree-like
            (5) **Groundpine**   *Lycopodium obscurum*
5. Leaves with pungent tips
            (3) **Bristly Clubmoss**   *Lycopodium annotinum*
5. Leaves with soft hair-like tips
            (4) **Running Clubmoss**   *Lycopodium clavatum*
   6. Sterile branches cylindrical; leaves uniform
            (6) **Alaska Clubmoss**   *Lycopodium sabinaefolium*

6. Sterile branches flattened; leaves of undersurface of branches reduced in size
(7) **Running Pine** *Lycopodium complanatum*

(1)   **Fir Clubmoss** *Lycopodium Selago* L. *L. Selago* is a common plant above treeline, the stems rising from the rootstocks in cylindrical clusters. The spikes characteristic of most clubmosses are lacking in this species, the sporangia being found at the bases of unmodified leaves. The species is circumboreal. Most New England material belongs to var. *Selago* which is characterized by having the leaves more or less appressed. Var. *patens* (Beauv.) Desv. with longer, widely spreading leaves may occasionally be found, but probably not above treeline. (Mountain clubmoss.) A fruiting plant is shown on Pl. 4, 1.

(2)   **Shining Clubmoss** *Lycopodium lucidulum* Michx. The Shining Clubmoss resembles the previous species in having the sporangia borne in leaf axils along the stem. The sporangia-bearing leaves are somewhat shorter than the other leaves giving the branches an uneven appearance. The species is common throughout our area in cool woods and extends well up on the mountains but ordinarily not above treeline. Its total range is from Newfoundland to Ontario and south to South Carolina, Tennessee and Missouri in the mountains. A fruiting plant is shown on Pl. 4, 2.

(3)   **Bristly Clubmoss** *Lycopodium annotinum* L. The erect stems of this species are stiff and simple or only sparingly branched. The sporangia are borne in spikes at the ends of leafy stems. The species is found throughout the cooler parts of the northern hemisphere. There are three intergrading varieties recognized. The commonest one in the subalpine regions is var. *pungens* (LaPylaie) Desv. in which the leaves are ascending or appressed and the leaf margins are only slightly if at all toothed. This species and *L. Selago* are the only ones commonly found above treeline in our area. (Stiff clubmoss, interrupted clubmoss.) A fruiting plant is shown on Pl. 4, 3.

(4)   **Running Clubmoss** *Lycopodium clavatum* L. *L. clavatum* is sometimes called pussy-toes because of its soft branches. The stems creep along the ground and give off short branches. The leaves are narrow and have slender bristles at their tips. The spikes are borne at the top of a long stalk which has scattered reduced leaves. A number of varieties are recognized, the one most likely to be found above treeline is var. *megastachyon* Fern. & Bissell in which the leaves are ascending or appressed and there is a single spike per stalk. The running clubmoss is a cosmopolitan species.

In our area the species is common in woods and thickets and on the mountains but it only occasionally gets above treeline. (Common clubmoss, staghorn-moss, staghorn evergreen, coral evergreen, buckhorn, wolf's-claws.) A fruiting plant is seen on Pl. 5, 1.

(5)   **Groundpine** *Lycopodium obscurum* L. The tree-like habit of the erect stems of this species distinguishes it from all the other clubmosses. There are two well-marked varieties; var. *obscurum* has the branches flattened or concave beneath while var. *dendroideum* (Michx.) D.C.Eat. has cylindric branches. Both varieties are common in our area and extend well up on the mountains but probably not above treeline. The species extends across the northern portion of North America and is also found in eastern Asia. (Flat-branch groundpine, round-branch groundpine, tree clubmoss, bunch evergreen.) A fruiting plant is seen on Pl. 4, 4.

(6)   **Alaska Clubmoss** *Lycopodium sabinaefolium* Willd., var. *sitchense* (Rupr.) Fern. The Alaska clubmoss is a relatively small species with the horizontal stem running close to the surface of the ground and erect stems which superficially resemble a somewhat reduced *L. annotinum*. The leaves are smaller and in fewer ranks around the stem. The bracts making up the spikes have slender spreading tips. The Alaska clubmoss occurs from Labrador to Alaska and is found on Katahdin, Mt. Washington and the Adirondacks. (Sitkan clubmoss, savin-leaved clubmoss, cedar-like clubmoss, groundfir, heath-cypress.) A fruiting plant is seen on p. 23, c.

(7)   **Running Pine** *Lycopodium complanatum* L., var. *flabelliforme* Fern. This is a familiar clubmoss, sometimes called lion's paw, and often used in Christmas greens. The leaves are in four ranks on the branches and are scale-like rather than needle-like, as in the other species. Several spikes are found at the tips of fertile branches. The species is found in dry woods throughout the northern hemisphere. While essentially a lowland species it also occurs well up on the mountains in the elfin forest, or krummholz. (Groundpine, trailing evergreen, groundcedar, Christmas green, creeping Jenny.) A fruiting plant is seen on Pl. 5, 3.

ISOËTACEAE (Quillwort Family)

The quillworts are a small group of aquatic plants growing on the mud at the bottom of shallow ponds and slow streams. Each plant consists of a cluster of quill-like leaves; sporangia, producing spores of two sizes, are contained in the leaf bases. All the species look very much alike and they are differentiated by studying the size and the sculpturing of the spores with a compound microscope. Quillworts are seldom collected since no one except a specialist in the group is likely to work up much enthusiasm for the genus.

Short-spined Quillwort *Isoëtes muricata* Dur. *I. muricata* has a range which extends from Greenland to Alaska and south to Pennsylvania, Colorado, and California. It is the only species one is likely to find in high mountain lakes such as the Lakes of the Clouds on Mt. Washington. A plant is shown on p. 21, a.

a. **Short-spined Quillwort**   b. **Red Spruce**   c. **Black Spruce**
   Isoëtes muricata   *Picea rubens*   *Picea mariana*

OSMUNDACEAE (Flowering Fern Family)

The *Osmundaceae* is separated from the *Polypodiaceae*, which contains most of our ferns, on rather technical differences in the structure of the sporangia. It is a small family containing only three genera and in North America it is represented by the genus *Osmunda* which contains the royal fern, the interrupted fern, and the cinnamon fern, all common species in our lowlands.

Interrupted Fern *Osmunda Claytoniana* L. In the interrupted fern most of the pinnae of the frond are sterile, but a few pairs near the middle of the frond are much modified and bear the sporangia, hence the common name. It is the largest of the ferns which grow above timberline and even if the fronds are entirely sterile the large lobed but untoothed pinnae are quite different from those of the other ferns to be expected there. The species occurs from Newfoundland to Manitoba and south to Georgia and Arkansas. A variety of this species is found in the Himalaya. While a common fern at lower elevations, it is not very abundant above treeline. A fruiting plant is seen on Pl. 6, 1.

POLYPODIACEAE (Fern Family)

This family includes most of our common ferns. The conspicuous leaf-like parts of ferns are known as *fronds*. The fronds may be divided into a number of divisions or *pinnae*; the pinnae are sometimes subdivided into a number of *pinnules*; and the pinnules may in turn be broken up into still smaller divisions. The reproductive bodies of the ferns are sporangia containing spores. The sporangia are grouped together into clusters, each cluster being called a *sorus* or fruit dot. The fruit dot is often covered when young by a protective membrane, the *indusium*. In most ferns the fruit dots are borne on the under surface (the back) of the frond.

1. Fronds at least half as broad as long . . . . 2.
1. Fronds less than half as broad as long . . . . 3.
  2. Seldom ten inches tall; basal pair of pinnae projected downward   (2) **Long Beech Fern** *Dryopteris Phegopteris*
  2. Usually more than a foot tall; basal pair of pinnae ascending   (7) **Bracken** *Pteridium latiusculum*
3. Fronds broadest at middle and tapering to apex and base . 4.
3. Fronds not tapering to base . . . . 5.
  4. Fronds bearing numerous conspicuous scales; fruit dots circular   (4) **Fragrant Fern** *Dryopteris fragrans*
  4. Fronds not scale-bearing; fruit dots elongate   (6) **Lady-Fern** *Athyrium Filix-femina*
5. Fronds bearing scales or chaff . . . . 6.
5. Fronds without scales or chaff . . . . 7.
  6. Fronds less than ten inches tall; pinnae lobed but not toothed   (1) **Rusty Woodsia** *Woodsia ilvensis*
  6. Fronds a foot or more tall; divisions of pinnae sharply toothed   (3) **Spinulose Woodfern** *Dryopteris spinulosa*
7. Pinnae much divided; fruit dots marginal   (5) **Hay-scented Fern** *Dennstaedtia punctilobula*
7. Pinnae not divided; fruit dots not marginal   (8) **Common Polypody** *Polypodium virginianum*

(1)   **Rusty Woodsia** *Woodsia ilvensis* (L.) R.Br. The common name of this fern is derived from the fact that the stem and under side of the frond are covered by hair-like scales which are silvery white at first but which later turn rusty brown. The stems are jointed about an inch above the rootstock and the fronds die early and break off at the joint leaving the persistent bases standing. This stubble serves to identify the fern. The rusty woodsia grows in crevices in cliffs and ledges exposed to the sun. It is circumboreal in its distribution and is fairly common in New Eng-

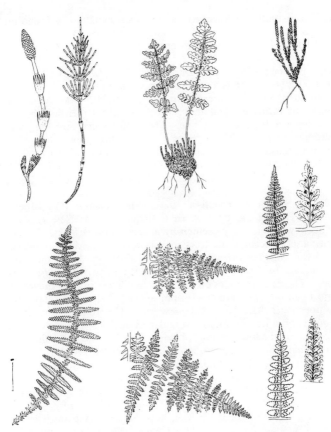

a. **Field Horsetail**
   Equisetum arvense

b. **Rusty Woodsia**
   Woodsia ilvensis

c. **Alaska Clubmoss**
   Lycopodium sabinaefolium,
   var. *sitchense*

d. **Fragrant Fern**
   Dryopteris fragrans

Spinulose Woodfern
Dryopteris spinulosa
e. Var. *intermedia*
   basal pinna

f. **Hay-scented Fern**
   Dennstaedtia punctilobula
   pinna and pinnule

g. Var. *americana*
   basal pinna

h. **Lady-Fern**
   Athyrium Filix-femina
   var. *Michauxii*
   pinna and pinnule

land as a species at lower elevations. Occasionally it is found on ledges fairly high on the mountains. (Fragrant Woodsia, rusty cliff-fern.) The plant is shown on Pl. 5, 2, and on p. 23, b.

(2) **Long Beech Fern** *Dryopteris Phegopteris* (L.) Christens. The long beech fern is a common New England fern, which seems quite at home above treeline in the mountains. The fronds are about six inches tall and are relatively broad for their length, giving them a triangular outline. The basal pinnae are long and strongly reflexed. This species is found throughout the cooler parts of the northern hemisphere; in North America it ranges from Newfoundland to Alaska, and southward to North Carolina in the mountains. (Northern beech fern.) A frond is shown on p. 26, a.

(3) **Spinulose Woodfern** *Dryopteris spinulosa* (O.F.Muell.) Watt. The spinulose woodfern is frequent in the New England woods, where it is represented by a number of varieties. Two of the varieties occur above treeline, var. *intermedia* (Muhl.) Underw. and var. *americana* (Fisch.) Fern., var. *americana* being the more common. In var. *intermedia* the frond is narrowly oblong-lanceolate. The basal pinnules on the upper and lower sides of the lowermost pair of pinnae are nearly opposite and the lower basal pinnule is not longer than the pinnule next to it. The frond of var. *americana* is broader and more triangular in outline. The lower basal pinnule on the lower pair of pinnae is $\frac{1}{4}$ to $\frac{3}{4}$ farther from the main stem than the basal upper pinnule and is decidedly longer than the one next to it. The fronds of var. *intermedia* are evergreen while those of var. *americana* are not. The species is circumboreal; var. *intermedia* is confined to the eastern half of North America, var. *americana* extends across the continent. (Toothed woodfern, spinulose shieldfern, fancy fern, florist's fern.) A plant is shown on Pl. 6, 2. A basal pinna of var. *intermedia* is shown above and var. *americana* below on p. 23, e, g.

(4) **Fragrant Fern** *Dryopteris fragrans* (L.) Schott, var. *remotiuscula* Komarov. The fragrant fern is rare in our area even in the lowlands and seldom occurs high on the mountains but it has been found near the summit of Mt. Mansfield. The fronds are evergreen and the shrivelled and curled old fronds persist for a long time about the base of the plant. The stipe of the frond bears numerous brownish scales and the pinnae are glandular and aromatic, the odor persisting for several years on herbarium specimens. As Tilton says, "When growing the fern may be tested by its fragrance, its stickiness and its beautiful brown curls." The fern

grows on shaded cliffs, often on limestone. The species is circum-boreal, the variety is found in eastern North America and eastern Asia. (Fragrant cliff-fern.) A frond is shown on p. 23, d.

(5) **Hay-scented Fern** *Dennstaedtia punctilobula* (Michx.) Moore. The hay-scented fern gets its name from the pleasant odor given off by the dry fronds. The fronds are of moderate height and are covered by hairs and small glands. The pinnae have about the same general outline in miniature as the entire frond. The pinnules are thin and delicately toothed. The fruit dots are close to the margins of the pinnules and the indusia are cup-shaped, enclosing the clusters of sporangia. The hay-scented fern is found where there is partial shade and sufficient moisture, throughout the eastern half of North America; in our area it is common at lower elevations and is occasionally found well up on the mountains. (Boulder fern, pasture fern.) A pinna and a pinnule are shown on p. 23, f.

(6) **Lady-Fern** *Athyrium Filix-femina* (L.) Roth, var. *Michauxii* (Spreng.) Farw. The lady-fern has fronds a foot or more tall rising from a rather thick rootstock. The fronds are lance-shaped and taper to the base as well as to the apex. The pinnae are also lance-shaped and are distinctly toothed. The fruit dots are elongate and partially covered by somewhat horseshoe-shaped indusia. When the fruit dots are mature, they almost cover the under surface of the frond with rust-colored sporangia. The lady-fern is a rather plastic species and a large number of varieties and forms have been described, many of which are rather difficult to separate and of doubtful value. The species is cosmopolitan and the variety is common in our area and is fairly frequent well up on the mountains. (Upland lady-fern, northern lady-fern.) A plant is shown on Pl. 5, 5; a pinna and a pinnule on p. 23, h.

(7) **Bracken** *Pteridium aquilinum* (L.) Kuhn, var. *latiusculum* (Desv.) Underw. The bracken is one of the most common ferns of our area. The fronds are broadly triangular in outline. The sporangia are borne in a continuous strip along the margins of the pinnules and the margin of the pinnule is bent over them and serves as an indusium. The species is cosmopolitan and the variety is found over much of North America and also occurs in Eurasia. While ordinarily a lowland species with us, it is occasionally found growing above 4000 feet on the mountains. (Eastern bracken, brake, pasture brake, hog-brake, eagle fern.) A young frond is shown on Pl. 6, 3; a mature frond on p. 26, b.

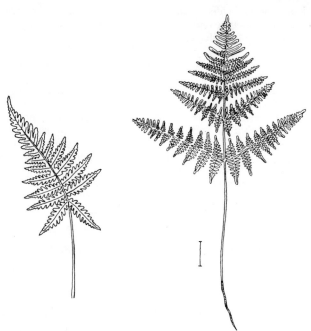

a. **Long Beech Fern**
 Dryopteris Phegopteris

b. **Bracken**
 Pteridium aquilinum, var. *latiusculum*

(8)   **Common Polypody** *Polypodium virginianum* L.   The
polypody is another of our very common ferns growing on ledges
and large boulders where there is only a suggestion of soil. The
evergreen fronds are divided into twelve to twenty pairs of untoothed
segments and the fruit dots are naked. *P. virginianum* occurs
from Newfoundland to British Columbia and south to Alabama,
and also in eastern Asia. It is very closely related to *P. vulgare*
of Europe and western America. Ordinarily a lowland species, it
reaches the summit ridge of Mt. Mansfield. (Rock polypody,
rockcap fern.) A plant is shown on Pl. 5, 4.

PINACEAE (Pine Family)

The pine family includes the conifers which are our most important timber trees. The conifers are seed-producing plants, but the
cones in which the seeds are borne are made up of sporophylls as
in the horsetails and clubmosses. The leaves are needle-like and

into blue berry-like structures with a white bloom. In northern New Hampshire the juniper is not common even at low elevations. A juniper has occasionally been collected above treeline on Katahdin and Mt. Washington. It is debatable whether these are plants of var. *depressa* which have been seeded there by birds or var. *saxatilis* Pallas, a very similar variety which is found on mountains in other parts of North America. (Ground juniper, dwarf juniper.) A branch is shown on Pl. 7, 1.

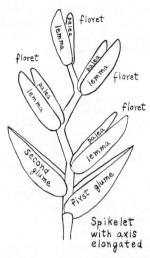

Spikelet with axis elongated

GRAMINEAE (Grass Family)

The habit of calling all turf-forming plants "grasses" is as deep-seated as that of referring to all conifers as "pines" and just as irritating to botanists. The turf above timberline is a mixture of grasses, sedges, and rushes with the sedges predominating. Superficially grasses and sedges look somewhat alike but the two are not difficult to tell apart.

The stems of grasses are usually round and hollow except for the hard nodes; the jointed stems are called *culms*. The leaves have basal sheaths surrounding the stem; the sheath is usually split on the side opposite the blade. At the junction of the sheath with the blade is a small collar-like structure called the *ligule*. Each flower of a grass is enclosed by two scale-like structures which are highly modified leaves. The outer scale is called the *lemma*, the inner the *palea*. The lemma, palea and enclosed flower make up a *floret*. From one to several florets are borne in two rows along a

29

short branch. At the base of the branch are a pair of sterile scales known as *glumes*. The glumes and florets on the branch make up a *spikelet*. The accompanying diagram may help clear up these points. The grass inflorescence is made up of a large number of spikelets. The inflorescence of most of the grasses here treated is a *panicle*; in *Agropyron* it is a spike, in *Phleum* a spike-like panicle, and in *Trisetum* the panicle is somewhat spike-like.

The grass family contains over four thousand species, but the number found above treeline in our area is relatively small so that the uplands are a good place to start learning them. A hand lens is almost necessary in studying the structure of the spikelets as is a millimeter ruler for taking measurements.

1. Awns present on either the glumes or the lemmas . . . . 2.
1. Awns not present on the glumes or the lemmas . . . . . 18.
   2. Inflorescence a dense cylindric or ovoid spike   . . . . 3.
   2. Inflorescence more diffuse . . . . 4.
3. Spike several times as long as broad; awn of glume short
                      (23) **Timothy**   *Phleum pratense*
3. Spike about twice as long as broad; awn of glume longer
             (24) **Alpine Timothy**   *Phleum alpinum*
   4. Spikelets one-flowered . . . . 5.
   4. Spikelets with two or more flowers . . . . 11.
5. Florets with a cluster of hairs at base . . . . 6.
5. Florets without hairs at base . . . . 10.
   6. Awn twisted at base, the tip protruding from the glumes 7.
   6. Awn straight or slightly arched, the tip not protruding
      from the glumes . . . . 9.
7. Hairs in two tufts, 3 mm. or less long . . . . 8.
7. Hairs in a continuous ring, 3–4 mm. long; only one collection known   (18) **Cloudy Reedgrass**   *Calamagrostis nubila*
   8. Hairs 1 mm. or less long
         (16) **Pickering Reedgrass**   *Calamagrostis Pickeringii*
   8. Hairs 3 mm. long
         (17) **Pond Reedgrass**   *Calamagrostis lacustris*
9. Inflorescence open; hairs of equal length
         (19) **Bluejoint**   *Calamagrostis canadensis*
9. Inflorescence contracted; hairs of two lengths
       (20) **Neglected Reedgrass**   *Calamagrostis neglecta*
10. Awn attached near summit of the lemma
       (22) **Drooping Woodreed**   *Cinna latifolia*
10. Awn attached near the middle of the lemma
       (21) **Boreal Bentgrass**   *Agrostis borealis*
11. Glumes much shorter than the rest of the spikelet . . . . 12.

11. Glumes about equalling or exceeding length of rest of
spikelet . . . . 14.
12. Inflorescence open; spikelets stalked . . . . 13.
12. Inflorescence a single terminal spike; spikelets sessile
(11) **Slender Wheatgrass** *Agropyron trachycaulum*
13. First glume 1-nerved, second 3-nerved; lemma lightly
nerved (1) **Fringed Brome** *Bromus ciliatus*
13. First glume 3-nerved, second 5-nerved; lemma strongly
7-nerved (2) **False Melic** *Schizachne purpurascens*
14. Spikelets two- or three-flowered . . . . 15.
14. Spikelets more than three-flowered
(15) **Poverty Oatgrass** *Danthonia spicata*
15. Spikelets two-flowered . . . . 16.
15. Spikelets three-flowered, the terminal floret perfect and
awnless, the lower two staminate, with awned lemmas
(26) **Alpine Sweetgrass** *Hierochloë alpina*
16. Inflorescence spike-like; the lemmas distinctly bidentate
at tip, the awn attached about one third below tip
(12) **Spiked Trisetum** *Trisetum spicatum*
16. Inflorescence more open; the awn attached near the base
of the lemma . . . . 17.
17. Glumes not exceeding the upper floret; the awn extending
some distance out of spikelet
(13) **Crinkled Hairgrass** *Deschampsia flexuosa*
17. Glumes exceeding the florets; awns barely protruding
(14) **Mountain Hairgrass** *Deschampsia atropurpurea*
18. Flowers modified into leafy tufts
(3) **Proliferous Fescue** *Festuca prolifera*
18. Flowers normal . . . . 19.
19. Glumes shorter than the lowest floret . . . . 20.
19. Glumes as long as the lowest floret
(25) **Sweetgrass** *Hierochloë odorata*
20. Glumes much shorter than the first floret; the florets
strongly parallel-nerved
(4) **Fowl Mannagrass** *Glyceria striata*
20. Glumes somewhat longer; the florets not strongly nerved 21.
21. Web at base of floret scant or wanting . . . . 22.
21. Web at base of floret well developed . . . . 24.
22. Culms from creeping rootstalks, not tufted; spikelets
three- to six-flowered (5) **Canada Bluegrass** *Poa compressa*
22. Without creeping rootstalks, culms tufted; spikelets two-
to four-flowered . . . . 23.
23. Plants moss-green, forming loose tufts
(10) **Wavy Bluegrass** *Poa Fernaldiana*

23. Plants with a whitish bloom; culms erect and rigid

(9) **Glaucous Bluegrass** *Poa glauca*

24. Lemma glabrous except for web at base

(7) **Thicket Bluegrass** *Poa saltuensis*

24. Lemma pubescent on keel and margin . . . . 25.

25. Culms from creeping rootstalks; nerves on lemmas distinct

(6) **Kentucky Bluegrass** *Poa pratensis*

25. Without creeping rootstalks; nerves on lemmas obscure

(8) **Wood Bluegrass** *Poa nemoralis*

(1)   **Fringed Brome** *Bromus ciliatus* L. The fringed brome has slender culms a yard or more tall. The panicle may be a foot long, with slender drooping branches. The spikelets are large and several-flowered; the glumes are shorter than the florets, the first is one-nerved, the second three-nerved; the lemmas are distinctly toothed at the tip with an awn arising from the notch and with hairy margins. The species is widespread in moist soils from Newfoundland to British Columbia, and in much of the United States except the southeastern states. It is usually a woodland species, but occasionally pushes up to treeline. A culm and enlarged spikelet are shown on p. 33, a.

(2)   **False Melic** *Schizachne purpurascens* (Torr.) Swallen. The false melic is another fairly tall grass which resembles somewhat the previous species. In the false melic the leaves are narrower; the spikelets are large but tend to be fewer-flowered; the glumes are short, the first is three-nerved, the second five-nerved; the lemmas are distinctly seven-nerved, toothed at the tip with a slightly divergent awn arising from the notch, the margins are not hairy. The species occurs in eastern Asia and from Newfoundland to Alaska and south to West Virginia and New Mexico. It is a species of rocky woodlands but it is occasionally found well up on the mountains. A culm and enlarged spikelet are shown on p. 33, b.

(3)   **Proliferous Fescue** *Festuca prolifera* (Piper) Fern. The proliferous fescue is a relatively low grass, growing in loose tufts from creeping rootstocks. The inflorescence is a simple raceme of three to thirteen spikelets. The spikelets are long and slender with most of the florets modified into leafy tufts. The species is restricted to the mountains of western Newfoundland, Anticosti Island, the Gaspé Peninsula, Katahdin, and Mt. Washington. It is not a common grass in our region. The species is perhaps better considered as a viviparous mountain form of *F. rubra*. A culm and enlarged spikelet are shown on p. 33, c.

a. **Fringed Brome**
   Bromus ciliatus

b. **False Melic**
   Schizachne purpurascens

c. **Proliferous Fescue**
   Festuca prolifera

d. **Fowl Mannagrass**
   Glyceria striata

(4) **Fowl Mannagrass** *Glyceria striata* (Lam.) Hitchc., var. *stricta* (Scribn.) Fern. The fowl mannagrass is pale green and forms tussocks, with culms 1–3 feet tall. The panicle is open with ascending branches; the usually purple spikelets are small and three- to seven-flowered; the glumes are very short; the lemmas are strongly seven-nerved and awnless. The variety is found from Labrador to Alaska and south to Long Island, South Dakota and northern Mexico. In our area it occasionally is found well up on the mountains. (Fowl meadowgrass.) A culm and enlarged spikelet are shown on p. 33, d.

(5) **Canada Bluegrass** *Poa compressa* L. The genus *Poa* is a large and rather difficult one. The Canada bluegrass has culms which are flattened, solitary or a few in a clump, up to 2 feet tall and of a bluish-green color. The panicle is narrow with the branches in pairs; the spikelets are about $\frac{1}{4}$ inch long; the glumes are about half the length of the spikelet; the lemmas have little or no web at the base and are only slightly hairy on the margins. This grass is often grown for pasturage in poor soil. In spite of its common name the species is a native of Europe, but has been widely planted in North America, where it is naturalized and is found from Newfoundland to Alaska and through most of the United States. It has been collected on the summit of Mt. Washington. (Flattened meadowgrass, wiregrass.) A culm and enlarged spikelet are shown on p. 35, a.

(6) **Kentucky Bluegrass** *Poa pratensis* L. The Kentucky bluegrass has culms which are round, tufted, and from 1–3 feet tall. The panicles are open with a number of branches at each joint; the spikelets are about the same size as in the previous species; the lemmas are distinctly webbed at the base and have silky hairs on the margins. This grass is extensively grown for lawns and for pasture where the soil is good. It is found, at least in lawns, over the entire United States. It was introduced from Europe over much of its range but it may be native in extreme northern United States and Canada. *P. pratensis* has been split into a number of subspecies and varieties. The apparently native form which is found above treeline is treated as a distinct species by some, as *P. alpigena* (Fries) Lindm. (Meadowgrass, Junegrass, speargrass.) A culm, enlarged spikelet, and enlarged floret are shown on p. 35, b.

(7) **Thicket Bluegrass** *Poa saltuensis* Fern. & Wieg. The thicket bluegrass grows in loose tufts with culms less than 3 feet tall. The panicle is open, with two or three nodding branches at each joint; the spikelets are three- to five-flowered; the lemmas

34

a. **Canada Bluegrass**
   Poa compressa

b. **Kentucky Bluegrass**
   Poa pratensis

c. **Thicket Bluegrass**
   Poa saltuensis

d. **Wood Bluegrass**
   Poa nemoralis

are not hairy on the margins, but have a well developed web at the base. The species is found from Newfoundland to Ontario, and in the United States from New England to Minnesota and south along the mountains to West Virginia. A culm, enlarged spikelet, and enlarged floret are shown on p. 35, c.

(8)   **Wood Bluegrass**   *Poa nemoralis* L. The wood bluegrass has tufted grass-green culms up to 2 feet tall. The panicle is open with spreading branches; the two- to five-flowered spikelets are relatively small; the glumes are narrow, sharp pointed and three-nerved; the lemmas are hairy along the margins and sparsely webbed at the base. The species is very variable and needs further study. It is widespread in Europe and temperate Asia; in North America its range extends from Labrador to Alaska and south to Delaware. In North America there is some question whether it is a native or introduced species; perhaps it is both. A culm, enlarged spikelet, and enlarged floret are shown on p. 35, d.

(9)   **Glaucous Bluegrass**   *Poa glauca* Vahl. The glaucous bluegrass, as the name implies, is covered by a whitish bloom; the culms are about a foot tall, in close or loose tufts. The panicle is narrow and compact, with ascending branches; the spikelets are two- to four-flowered and small; the glumes are broader and less distinctly nerved than in *P. nemoralis*; the lemmas are hairy on the lower half of the keel and the obscure nerves but there is no web at the base. The species is circumboreal in cold regions and extends southward along the mountains into the United States. Like many other *Poas* the species needs further study. A culm, enlarged spikelet, and enlarged floret are shown on p. 37, a.

(10)   **Wavy Bluegrass**   *Poa Fernaldiana* Nannf. The wavy bluegrass is a low, matted alpine with slender flexuous culms growing in loose bunches less than a foot tall. The panicle is narrow, but loose, with few spikelets borne near the tips of the ascending branches; the spikelets are two- to four-flowered; the glumes are lanceolate; the lemmas are hairy on the lower half of the keel and marginal nerves and the bases are sparsely if at all webbed. The range of the species extends from northern Labrador to the mountains of our area. A culm, enlarged spikelet, and enlarged floret are shown on p. 37, b.

(11)   **Slender   Wheatgrass**   *Agropyron   trachycaulum*   (Link) Malte. The slender wheatgrass is usually less than 2 feet tall. The inflorescence is a slender spike up to a foot long; the spikelets are large and several-flowered; the glumes are five- to seven-nerved and pointed at the tip or bearing a short awn; the lemmas are also

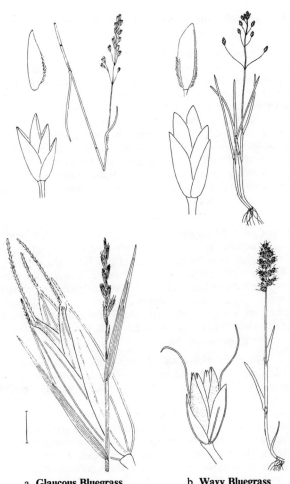

a. **Glaucous Bluegrass**
   Poa glauca

b. **Wavy Bluegrass**
   Poa Fernaldiana

c. **Slender Wheatgrass**
   Agropyron trachycaulum

d. **Spiked Trisetum**
   Trisetum spicatum

nerved and bear somewhat longer awns at their tips. The species occurs over much of Canada and the United States except for the southeastern states. The species is divided into a number of varieties; most of the mountain collections are either var. *majus* (Vasey) Fern. with the glume, excluding the awn, $\frac{1}{2}$ inch long or var. *novae-*

angliae (Scribn.) Fern. with the body of the glume $\frac{1}{3}$ inch long. A culm and enlarged spikelet are shown on p. 37, c.

(12)   **Spiked Trisetum**   *Trisetum spicatum* (L.) Richter. The spiked trisetum grows in dense tufts, with culms up to 2 feet tall. The panicle is dense and spike-like; the spikelets are usually two-flowered; the first glume is narrow and one-nerved, the second broader and three-nerved; the lemmas are notched at the tip and bear a spreading awn attached about one third below the tip. The species is circumboreal and occurs in the mountains of Mexico and southern South America. It is a very variable species and numerous varieties have been described. Our material usually belongs to var. *pilosiglume* Fern. which has pilose glumes. The variety is found from Labrador to the north shore of Lake Superior and south to the mountains of New England and Minnesota. A culm and enlarged spikelet are shown on p. 37, d.

(13)   **Crinkled Hairgrass**   *Deschampsia flexuosa* (L.) Trin. The crinkled hairgrass grows in dense tufts, with culms up to a yard tall. The panicle is loose, open, and nodding; the spikelets are two-flowered; the glumes are thin, pointed, and shorter than the florets; the lemmas bear long twisted awns attached near the base. The species is circumboreal and is usually found on relatively dry soils. In the United States it is chiefly confined to the eastern states. (Common hairgrass, wavy hairgrass.) A culm and enlarged spikelet are shown on p. 39, a.

(14)   **Mountain Hairgrass**   *Deschampsia atropurpurea* (Wahlenb.) Scheele. The mountain hairgrass is about the same height as the previous species, but grows in looser tufts. The panicle is loose and open, with relatively few branches; the spikelets are purplish; the glumes are much longer than the florets; the awns are attached near the middle of the lemmas and are almost hidden by the long glumes. The species is circumboreal in cool bogs and meadows. In the United States, the species is confined to the mountains of the Northeast and the West. (Purple hairgrass.) A culm and enlarged spikelet are shown on p. 39, b.

(15)   **Poverty Oatgrass**   *Danthonia spicata* (L.) Beauv. The poverty oatgrass is usually not more than 2 feet tall, the basal leaves are curled but those of the culm are erect. The panicle has short branches each bearing one spikelet; the spikelets are several-flowered; the glumes are longer than the florets; the lemmas are two-toothed at the tip with a long twisted awn attached between the teeth. The species is found on dry, sterile soil from Newfoundland to British Columbia; in the United States it is general east

a. **Crinkled Hairgrass**
   Deschampsia flexuosa

b. **Mountain Hairgrass**
   Deschampsia atropurpurea

c. **Poverty Oatgrass**
   Danthonia spicata

d. **Pickering Reedgrass**
   Calamagrostis Pickeringii

of the Mississippi, and in the mountains of the West to New Mexico. While not a mountain species a number of collections have been made well up on Mt. Washington. (Poverty grass, white oatgrass, Junegrass). A plant and enlarged spikelet are shown on p. 39, c.

(16) **Pickering Reedgrass** *Calamagrostis Pickeringii* Gray. In the genus *Calamagrostis* we have five species which are separated by rather inconspicuous characters. The Pickering reedgrass is about a yard tall. The panicle is purplish, contracted and dense; the spikelets are one-flowered as in all the species; the glumes are sharp-pointed and almost completely smooth; the lemma is rough with an awn attached near its base and the awn is twisted so that it protrudes from the side of the spikelet; at the base of the lemma are two tufts of hairs which are less than one millimeter long. The species occurs from Labrador and Newfoundland to the mountains of New England and New York. Var. *debilis* (Kearney) Fern. & Wieg. is a smaller, more slender plant with somewhat smaller spikelets. It has a similar range but grows at lower elevations and extends south to Massachusetts and New Jersey. A culm, enlarged spikelet, and enlarged floret are shown on p. 39, d.

(17) **Pond Reedgrass** *Calamagrostis lacustris* (Kearney) Nash. *C. lacustris* looks very much like *C. Pickeringii*. It differs in having rougher glumes, thinner lemmas and basal hairs 3 millimeters long. It occurs from Labrador to northern Ontario and south to New Hampshire, Vermont, New York and Minnesota. It grows in damp soil well up on the mountains. An enlarged spikelet and floret are shown on p. 41, b.

(18) **Cloudy Reedgrass** *Calamagrostis nubila* Louis-Marie. This species is known from a single collection made by William Boott at the Lakes of the Clouds on Mt. Washington in 1862. It differs from the two previous species in having the long hairs at the base of the lemma form a continuous ring instead of being in two tufts. This species is not illustrated since there seems little chance that it will ever be found again.

(19) **Bluejoint** *Calamagrostis canadensis* (Michx.) Nutt. Bluejoint is a tall grass, plants in the lowlands sometimes being higher than a man's head. The panicle is purplish and varies in density and compactness; the awn of the lemma is straight and short, being hidden by the glumes; the hairs at the base of the lemma equal or exceed the lemma and are of uniform length. The species occurs over much of Canada and the United States. A number of varieties

a. **Bluejoint**
   Calamagrostis
   canadensis,
   var. *robusta*

b. **Pond Reedgrass**
   Calamagrostis
   lacustris
   spikelet and floret

c. **Boreal Bentgrass**
   Agrostis borealis

d. **Bluejoint**
   Calamagrostis
   canadensis,
   var. *scabra*

e. **Neglected Reedgrass**
   Calamagrostis
   neglecta
   spikelet and floret

f. **Drooping Woodreed**
   Cinna latifolia

are recognized, most of the mountain collections being var. *robusta* Vasey or var. *scabra* (Presl) Hitchc. The spikelets of var. *scabra* are larger than those of var. *robusta*. The glumes of var. *scabra* are usually ciliate along the keel and short pubescent elsewhere while those of var. *robusta* are merely roughened along the keel and elsewhere. A culm and enlarged spikelet of var. *robusta* and var. *scabra* are seen on p. 41, a, d.

(20)   **Neglected Reedgrass**   *Calamagrostis neglecta* (Ehrh.) Gaertn., Mey. & Scherb. In general appearance *C. neglecta* resembles *C. Pickeringii*. It differs in having a short straight awn hidden by the glumes and in having the hairs about the lemma of unequal lengths. The species is circumboreal and extends southward into northern New England and New York where it has been collected high on Mt. Marcy. It also occurs in the mountains of the West. (Narrow small-reed.) An enlarged spikelet and floret are shown on p. 41, e.

(21)   **Boreal Bentgrass**   *Agrostis borealis* Hartm. The boreal bentgrass grows in tufts which are less than 2 feet tall. The panicle is loose and spreading; the one-flowered spikelets are small; the glumes are narrowly ovate and about equal in length; the lemma nearly equals the glumes in length and bears near its middle a bent awn. The species is restricted to high latitudes and high altitudes. It is circumboreal in its distribution and in the United States is restricted to the Appalachian uplands of New England and New York. Robust plants which are taller, have broader leaves and larger spikelets have been segregated as var. *americana* (Scribn.) Fern. The variety is found from Newfoundland to New England, with an isolated station on the summit of Roan Mountain in North Carolina. A plant and enlarged spikelet are shown on p. 41, c.

(22)   **Drooping Woodreed**   *Cinna latifolia* (Trev.) Griseb. The drooping woodreed is a slender grass about 3 feet tall with a loose spreading, and often drooping panicle. The spikelet is one-flowered; the thin glumes are nearly equal; the lemma bears a short awn attached just below its tip. The species usually grows in moist woods and is circumboreal in its distribution. In the United States it is found from coast to coast in the northern states and in the mountains south to North Carolina, New Mexico, and central California. A culm and enlarged spikelet are shown on p. 41, f.

(23)   **Timothy**   *Phleum pratense* L. Timothy is one of the few grasses known to the average layman, either as timothy or herd's grass. It is our most important hay grass. The plant is often 3 feet

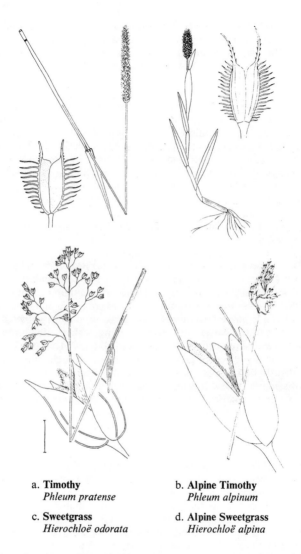

a. **Timothy**
   Phleum pratense

b. **Alpine Timothy**
   Phleum alpinum

c. **Sweetgrass**
   Hierochloë odorata

d. **Alpine Sweetgrass**
   Hierochloë alpina

tall, each culm terminating in a long spike-like panicle. The one-flowered spikelets are relatively small; the glumes are equal and completely hide the floret, each glume terminates in a stout awn and is ciliate along the keel. The species is native to Eurasia but has been widely cultivated throughout the temperate parts of the world and has frequently escaped and naturalized itself. Its occurrence on Mt. Washington dates back to the stagecoach days. (Cat's-tail, English hay.) A culm and enlarged spikelet are shown on p. 43, a.

(24)   **Alpine Timothy** *Phleum alpinum* L. The alpine timothy is seldom more than 2 feet tall, the upper leaf sheaths on the culms are inflated, and the inflorescence is rarely more than twice as long as broad and hence is elliptical rather than cylindrical. The awns on the glumes are longer and more slender than those of the previous species. It is native to the arctic and the alpine regions of both the Northern and Southern Hemispheres. In the United States it is found locally on the mountains of New England, northern Michigan, and the mountains of the West, where it serves as forage in the high range. A plant and enlarged spikelet are shown on p. 43, b.

(25)   **Sweetgrass** *Hierochloë odorata* (L.) Beauv. Sweetgrass is about 2 feet tall and the large spikelets are in open panicles. Each spikelet contains three florets, the lower two are staminate or sterile while the upper one is perfect; the glumes are broad and subequal; the sterile lemmas are awnless. This grass used to be gathered by the Indians and woven into sweet-smelling baskets. In Europe it was strewn before church doors on festival days. It is also known as vanilla grass, Seneca grass, and holy grass. It is circumboreal in its distribution but seldom found north of the Arctic Circle. It grows south to New Mexico and Arizona along the Rocky Mountains. Small prairies in the Yukon are carpeted with this grass in July. It is common in bogs and wet meadows in our area but above treeline is not as common as the next species. (Indian grass.) A culm and enlarged spikelet are shown on p. 43, c.

(26)   **Alpine Sweetgrass** *Hierochloë alpina* (Sw.) R. & S. The alpine sweetgrass is a shorter plant, the panicles are more compact, and the lemmas of the staminate florets bear awns attached below the tip. It is more arctic and alpine in its distribution than the previous species, being found far north of the Arctic Circle on Ellesmere Island and Greenland. It is circumboreal in its distribution; the mountains of New England and New York are its southern limit in North America. The Greenland and New England material has recently been separated from *H. alpina* and described as a new species *H. orthantha* by Thorvald Sorensen. An inflorescence and enlarged spikelet are shown on p. 43, d.

CYPERACEAE (Sedge Family)

The sedges differ from the grasses in various ways. The culms are often angular rather than round and in cross-section they are solid instead of hollow. The leaf sheaths are tubular, not split, and there is no ligule at the base of the blade. Each flower and fruit is subtended by a single scale and the flowers are usually arranged spirally. Sedges in flower are difficult to identify and mature specimens with well developed fruit should be selected for study. The mature fruits are hard seed-like structures called *achenes*. While small, their shapes when observed with the aid of a hand lens are so characteristic that they are of great importance in identification. In *Scirpus* and *Eriophorum* the achene is surrounded by a series of bristles. *Carex* is a large and difficult genus and even in the alpine area here treated nearly as many species are present as in the whole grass family. In *Carex* perianth bristles are lacking but the achene is enclosed in a papery sac, the *perigynium*. The shape and size of the mature perigynium is important in classifying specimens. The perigynium must be removed to study the achene.

1. Achene surrounded by bristles . . . . 2.
1. Achene enclosed in a papery perigynium . . . . . *Carex* 5.
  2. Inflorescence a single terminal spike . . . . 3.
  2. Inflorescence made up of many spikelets . . . . . . 4.
3. Low plants with small spikes; bristles surrounding achene
    inconspicuous   (1) **Deer's Hair** *Scirpus cespitosus*
3. Taller plants with larger spikes and conspicuous cotton-like
    bristles   (4) **Hare's Tail** *Eriophorum spissum*
  4. Achenes lens-shaped; bristles relatively short with mi-
    nute recurved barbs
        (2) **Red-tinged Bulrush** *Scirpus rubrotinctus*
  4. Achenes three-sided; bristles long, smooth, and much
    curled   (3) **Black-banded Wool-grass** *Scirpus atrocinctus*
5. Spike, one on each culm . . . . 6.
5. Spikes, two or more on each culm . . . . 8.
  6. Perigynia glabrous; spikes containing both staminate
    and pistillate flowers . . . . 7.
  6. Perigynia very hairy; some plants bearing only staminate
    spikes, others only pistillate spikes
        (13) **Scirpus-like Sedge** *Carex scirpoidea*
7. Spike somewhat globose; perigynia divergent, broadly egg-
    shaped; achenes lens-shaped
        (5) **Capitate Sedge** *Carex capitata*
7. Spike elongate; perigynia ascending, oblong; achene
    three-sided   (12) **Delicate Sedge** *Carex leptalea*

8. Achenes lens-shaped . . . . 9.
8. Achenes three-sided . . . . 17.
9. Spikes containing both staminate and pistillate flowers, not
   stalked . . . . 10.
9. Terminal spike all or mostly staminate, stalked . . . . . 15.
10. Perigynia lance-shaped, winged on the margin . . . . 14.
10. Perigynia neither lance-shaped nor winged on the margin 11.
11. Spikes per culm four or more, each bearing more than five
    perigynia . . . . 12.
11. Spikes per culm usually two, each bearing two to five peri-
    gynia   (6) **Three-seeded Sedge**   *Carex trisperma*
12. Perigynium with rounded margins; the achene nearly
    filling the perigynium . . . . 13.
12. Perigynium with thin margins; the achene occupying the
    upper half of the perigynium
                          (9) **Slender Sedge**   *Carex angustior*
13. Spikes and foliage gray-green, covered by a bloom; peri-
    gynia ten to thirty per spike; beak of perigynium incon-
    spicuous   (7) **Silvery Sedge**   *Carex canescens*
13. Spikes and foliage green, without a bloom; perigynia five
    to ten per spike; beak of perigynium distinct
                          (8) **Brownish Sedge**   *Carex brunnescens*
14. Plants 1–3 feet tall; main leaves at least $\frac{1}{4}$ inch wide;
    the lower spikes of the inflorescence scattered
                          (10) **Blunt Broom Sedge**   *Carex projecta*
14. Plants usually shorter; main leaves narrower; spikes of
    the inflorescence crowded
                      (11) **Crawford's Broom Sedge**   *Carex Crawfordii*
15. Spikelets borne on long, slender, often drooping stalks;
    scales narrow, with a distinct awn
                          (17) **Long-haired Sedge**   *Carex crinita*
15. Spikelets not on long slender stalks; scales broad and awn-
    less . . . . 16.
16. Perigynia smooth, nerveless; scales as long as the peri-
    gynia   (18) **Bigelow's Sedge**   *Carex Bigelowii*
16. Perigynia minutely granular, with brown nerves; scales
    about half as long as the perigynia
                  (19) **White Mountain Sedge**   *Carex lenticularis*
17. Perigynia pubescent . . . . 18.
17. Perigynia not pubescent . . . . 20.
18. Culms all long; spikes evident . . . . 19.
18. Culms of different lengths; spikes of short culms more or
    less hidden by leaf-sheaths
                          (16) **Woodland Sedge**   *Carex deflexa*

19. Mature leaves $\frac{1}{8}$ to $\frac{1}{4}$ inch broad; culms well overtopping the leaves; body of perigynium globose

(14) **Colonial Sedge**   *Carex communis*

19. Mature leaves $\frac{1}{16}$ inch or less wide; culms overtopped by leaves; body of perigynium oval

(15) **New England Sedge**   *Carex novae-angliae*

20. Perigynia beakless . . . . 21.
20. Perigynia distinctly beaked . . . . 23.
21. Scales about as long and wide as perigynia, not slender-pointed . . . . 22.
21. Scales narrow, longer than perigynia, long slender-pointed

(23) **Very Depauperate Sedge**   *Carex paupercula*

22. Scales enclosing the perigynia, soon falling

(21) **Few-flowered Sedge**   *Carex rariflora*

22. Scales not enclosing the perigynia, persistent

(22) **Quagmire Sedge**   *Carex limosa*

23. Achenes beakless . . . . 24.
23. Achenes with distinct beaks formed from persistent style bases; perigynia large and often inflated . . . . 29.
24. Bract at base of inflorescence sheathless; scales deep purple-brown; perigynia also dark colored

(20)   **Black Sedge**   *Carex atratiformis*

24. Bract at base of inflorescence with a distinct sheath; scales light-colored . . . . 25.
25. Spikes borne on distinct stalks . . . . 26.
25. Spikes sessile or on very short stalks; perigynia divergent

(28) **Yellowish Sedge**   *Carex flava*

26. Plants more then 10 inches tall; spikelets elongate, ten or more flowered . . . . 27.
26. Plants less than 10 inches tall; spikelets short, six- to eight-flowered   (26) **Hair-like Sedge**   *Carex capillaris*
27. Scales broader below than above; spikes spreading or drooping . . . . 28.
27. Scales broader above than below, sometimes awned; spikes ascending   (27) **Finely-nerved Sedge**   *Carex leptonervia*
28. Scales terminating in a tooth or short awn; perigynia obviously three-sided; achene near base of perigynium

(24) **Drooping Wood Sedge**   *Carex arctata*

28. Scales not terminating in a tooth or awn; perigynia obscurely three-sided; achene occupying midportion of perigynium   (25) **Slender-stalked Sedge**   *Carex debilis*
29. Perigynia spreading, gradually tapering to a long beak . . 30.
29. Perigynia ascending, egg-shaped to globose with a short beak . . . . 31.

30. Perigynia slender, only slightly inflated; leaves $\frac{1}{4}$ inch or
less broad   (29) **Michaux's Sedge**   *Carex Michauxiana*
30. Perigynia broader, much inflated; leaves usually more
than $\frac{1}{4}$ inch broad   (30) **Inflated Sedge**   *Carex intumescens*
31. Spikes cylindric, many flowered; leaves broad
(31) **Beaked Sedge**   *Carex rostrata*
31. Spikes globular, three- to fifteen-flowered; leaves narrow
(32) **Few-seeded Sedge**   *Carex oligosperma*

(1)   **Deer's Hair**   *Scirpus cespitosus* L., var. *callosus* Bigel.
Deer's hair is a low densely tufted sedge which makes up much
of the turf on moist soil above timberline. The spikes are small
and brown. The achenes are very small but with the aid of a hand
lens they can be seen to be three-sided and surrounded by six short
bristles. The species is common in the Arctic and the cool portions
of the Northern Hemisphere. The variety is found from Labrador
to Alaska and south to the mountains of Georgia and Utah. The
common name is one applied to the plant in England. (Tussock
Bulrush.) A plant is shown on Pl. 7, 3. A plant and enlarged
achene are illustrated on p. 49, a.

(2)   **Red-tinged Bulrush**   *Scirpus rubrotinctus* Fern. The red-
tinged bulrush gets its name from the characteristic coloration of
the leaf sheaths. It is a tall sedge with a large inflorescence. The
achenes are small and lens-shaped and they are hidden behind the
dark-colored scales. The bristles are relatively short and bear tiny
recurved barbs. It is a common sedge in low damp ground from
Labrador to Saskatchewan and south to New England, West Virginia and Nebraska. It has been collected on the summit of Mt.
Clinton and may occur on other mountains. An inflorescence and
enlarged achene are shown on p. 49, c.

(3)   **Black-banded Wool-grass**   *Scirpus atrocinctus* Fern. The
black-banded wool-grass is named for the dark color of the base
of the inflorescence and its subdivisions. It is a tall species with
three-sided achenes. The bristles are much longer than the scales,
drab in color and very conspicuous in the mature plant. It is a
common species in meadows and swamps from Newfoundland to
Washington and south to West Virginia and Iowa. It has been
found at 5000 feet on Mt. Washington. An inflorescence and an
enlarged achene are shown on p. 49, d.

(4)   **Hare's Tail**   *Eriophorum spissum* Fern. The hare's tail is
a typical cotton-grass with conspicuous white bristles which contrast sharply with the lead-colored scales. The stem is tall and triangular and surrounded by inflated and bladeless leaf sheaths. It

a. **Deer's Hair**
   Scirpus cespitosus, var. *callosus*

b. **Hare's Tail**
   Eriophorum spissum

c. **Red-tinged Bulrush**
   Scirpus rubrotinctus

d. **Black-banded Wool-grass**
   Scirpus atrocinctus

is common in cold bogs and on mountains from Baffin Island to Alaska and south to Pennsylvania and Minnesota. It is occasional in our area above treeline. An inflorescence is shown on Pl. 7, 4; an entire plant on p. 49, b.

49

(5)   **Capitate Sedge** *Carex capitata* L. The capitate sedge is a small species with very narrow leaves and single heads which terminate the culms. The perigynia are thin, white, almost nerveless, and distinctly beaked. The scales are thin, broad, and shorter than the perigynia. The species is a true arctic-alpine found throughout the Arctic and south to Mt. Washington, and along the Rocky Mountains to Mexico. It is also found in the southern Andes and Tierra del Fuego. A plant and an enlarged perigynium and scale are shown on p. 51, a.

(6)   **Three-seeded Sedge** *Carex trisperma* Dew. The three-seeded sedge is a weak slender species whose culms bear two or occasionally three small few-flowered spikes. The perigynia are oval with many fine nerves. The scales are ovate, sharp tipped, and slightly shorter than the perigynia. The species is found in mossy woods and bogs from Labrador to Saskatchewan and south to the mountains of North Carolina, Tennessee and Minnesota. While occurring in the woods of our area well up on the mountains it does not seem to get above treeline. A plant and an enlarged perigynium and scale are shown on p. 51, b.

(7)   **Silvery Sedge** *Carex canescens* L. The silvery sedge is a slender plant of medium height which forms loose stools in bogs and alpine meadows. The spikes are relatively small and the lower ones in the inflorescence tend to be somewhat scattered. The small perigynia are broadest below the middle, nerved, and not winged. The scales are also broad and somewhat shorter than the perigynia. The common name comes from the whitish bloom on the perigynia and foliage. The species is circumboreal in cool damp areas. A number of varieties are recognized but the alpine material belongs to var. *canescens*, the typical form. A plant and an enlarged perigynium and scale are shown on p. 51, c.

(8)   **Brownish Sedge** *Carex brunnescens* (Pers.) Poir. The brownish sedge resembles the previous species but lacks the bloom and has a deep green or brownish cast to the plant. The spikes are smaller, more globose, and fewer flowered than those of *C. canescens*. The perigynia are more distinctly beaked and the scales are broadest at the base rather than near the middle. The species is an arctic and alpine plant which is circumboreal in its distribution. Var. *sphaerostachya* (Tuckerm.) Kükenth. is a more flexuous form with more scattered spikes. It too is circumboreal but grows mostly at lower elevations and extends south to North Carolina whereas var. *brunnescens* goes only to New England and New York. A plant and an enlarged perigynium and scale are shown on p. 51, d.

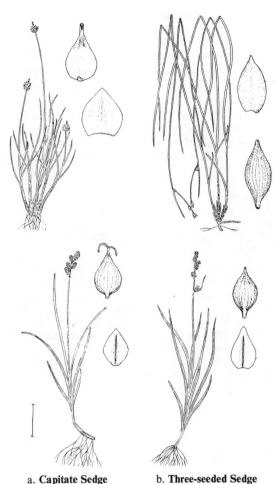

a. **Capitate Sedge**
   Carex capitata

b. **Three-seeded Sedge**
   Carex trisperma

c. **Silvery Sedge**
   Carex canescens

d. **Brownish Sedge**
   Carex brunnescens

(9)   **Slender Sedge**   *Carex angustior* Mackenz. *C. angustior* is
a small slender species with narrow leaves. The inflorescence is
made up of a small number of spikes, often only one or two, with
divergent perigynia. The perigynia are more or less lance-shaped
and the achene occupies the upper half of the perigynium instead

of nearly filling it. The scales are ovate, sharp pointed and about equal in length to the perigynia. The species is found in swales and damp thickets from Labrador to British Columbia and south to North Carolina and California. It is chiefly a sedge of the lowlands but it does occasionally occur above 4000 feet on the mountains of our area. A plant and an enlarged perigynium and scale are shown on p. 53, a.

(10) **Blunt Broom Sedge** *Carex projecta* Mackenz. This and the next species are two of a number of closely related species which even experts in the genus find difficult to separate. *C. projecta* is a fairly tall species with a somewhat elongate inflorescence in which the lower spikes are scattered. The perigynia are longer than the scales, are flattened, and have winged margins. The species occurs in damp ground from Newfoundland to British Columbia and south to West Virginia and Missouri. It is not an alpine species but seems to be the most common member of this group at fairly high elevations on our mountains. A culm and an enlarged perigynium and scale are shown on p. 53, b.

(11) **Crawford's Broom Sedge** *Carex Crawfordii* Fern. This species was named in honor of Ethan Allen Crawford. It is a smaller plant than the previous species, the leaves are narrower and the spikes of the inflorescence are more densely crowded. The perigynia resemble those of *C. projecta* but are somewhat smaller and plumper. This species is found throughout Canada and south to the mountains of Tennessee in the East. The species is common in our area in both moist and dry soil at low elevations but on the mountains it is less frequent than the previous species. A culm and an enlarged perigynium and scale are shown on p. 53, c.

(12) **Delicate Sedge** *Carex leptalea* Wahlenb. The delicate sedge is a slender rather inconspicuous species; each culm terminates in a single short and narrow spike. The perigynia are elliptical in outline; the scales are broad and shorter than the perigynia. It is a species of wet woods and bogs over much of Canada and the United States. It is occasionally found at elevations of over 4000 feet in our area. A plant and an enlarged perigynium and scale are shown on p. 53, d.

(13) **Scirpus-like Sedge** *Carex scirpoidea* Michx. The Scirpus-like sedge has the male and female flowers borne on separate plants. The stems are stiff and terminate in single cylindrical spikes. The ovoid perigynia are hairy and are longer than the purple scales. It is a circumboreal arctic-alpine species which occasionally is found at lower elevations; there was formerly a colony along the railroad

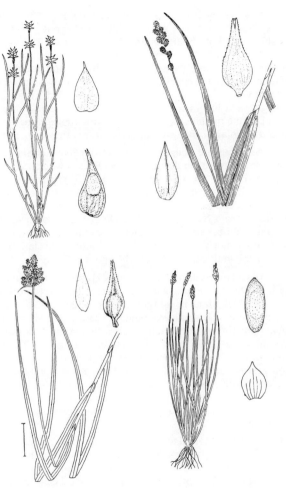

a. **Slender Sedge**
   Carex angustior

b. **Blunt Broom Sedge**
   Carex projecta

c. **Crawford's Broom Sedge**
   Carex Crawfordii

d. **Delicate Sedge**
   Carex leptalea

tracks north of Crawford Notch. The name is not a happy choice as the plant looks much more like an *Eleocharis* than a *Scirpus*. A plant and an enlarged perigynium and scale are shown on p. 55, a.

(14)   **Colonial Sedge**   *Carex communis* Bailey. The colonial sedge is a tussock-forming species with leaves about $\frac{1}{4}$ inch wide. The culms are all of about the same height and each bears several spikes. The body of the hairy perigynium is globose. The scales are of about the same length as the perigynia and usually have purplish margins. The species is found in woods and clearings from Quebec to Ontario and south to upland Georgia and Arkansas. It usually grows at low or moderate elevations but may occasionally be found on the mountains, but probably not above timberline. A plant and an enlarged perigynium and scale are shown on p. 55, b.

(15)   **New England Sedge**   *Carex novae-angliae* Schwein. This is a smaller and more slender species than the last with leaves which overtop the culms. The spikes per culm are fewer; the body of the perigynium is oval; the scales are shorter than the perigynia and terminate in sharp points. The species is found in woodlands and damp slopes from Newfoundland to Ontario and south to Pennsylvania and Wisconsin. While chiefly a lowland species it is occasionally found fairly well up on the mountains. A plant and an enlarged perigynium and scale are shown on p. 55, c.

(16)   **Woodland Sedge**   *Carex deflexa* Hornem. The woodland sedge is related to the previous two species. The plant produces long culms which about equal the leaves in height and short culms which are more or less hidden in the leaf bases. The short-beaked perigynia are abruptly contracted below the middle into a distinct stipe. The broad scales are shorter than the perigynia. The species is found in woods and on turfy slopes from Newfoundland to the Yukon and south to New England, New York and Minnesota. While ordinarily found at lower elevations it does occur on the alpine areas of Katahdin and Mt. Washington. A plant, an enlarged inflorescence, and an enlarged perigynium and scale are shown on p. 55, d.

(17)   **Long-haired Sedge**   *Carex crinita* Lam., var. *simulans* Fern. This is a tall coarse sedge with broad leaves that have rough margins. The spikes are long and slender and are borne on long drooping stalks. The perigynia, except for the beak, are almost orbicular in outline and somewhat inflated. The scales are much narrower and longer than the perigynia and terminate in distinct awns. The species is found in damp ground from Newfoundland to Manitoba and south over much of the eastern United States. It is a highly variable species and a number of varieties are recognized. The mountain material from our area belongs to var. *simulans*. The upper portion of a culm and an enlarged perigynium and scale are shown on p. 57, a.

a. **Scirpus-like Sedge**
   Carex scirpoidea
c. **New England Sedge**
   Carex novae-angliae
b. **Colonial Sedge**
   Carex communis
d. **Woodland Sedge**
   Carex deflexa

(18)   **Bigelow's Sedge** *Carex Bigelowii* Torr. This sedge is named in honor of Jacob Bigelow, physician, botanist and early White Mountain explorer. Bigelow Lawn is also named in his honor. Bigelow's sedge is fairly tall with relatively broad leaves. The spikes are stout and cylindric. The perigynia are usually pur- plish. The scales are about the same length as the perigynia and

55

brown or purplish black. Thus the species can be easily recognized by the dark color of the spikes. The species is found from Greenland to Baffin Island and Alaska and south to the alpine regions of New England and New York. A plant and an enlarged perigynium and scale are shown on p. 57, b.

(19) **White Mountain Sedge** *Carex lenticularis* Michx., var. *albi-montana* Dew. The White Mountain sedge is a moderately tall species with conspicuous cylindrical spikes. The perigynia are minutely granular and distinctly nerved. The scales are about half the length of the perigynia and purple-black with a broad green central stripe. The species ranges from Labrador to British Columbia and south to Massachusetts, New York and Idaho. The variety is found in the mountains of northern Labrador, Newfoundland, the Gaspé Peninsula and the White Mountains. The upper portion of a culm and an enlarged perigynium and scale are shown on p. 57, c.

(20) **Black Sedge** *Carex atratiformis* Britt. The black sedge is a slender species with drooping elliptical spikes borne on slender stalks. The perigynia are thin, nerveless, and short-beaked. The scales are about as long as the perigynia and purple-black with no green stripe. It is an alpine species found from Labrador to the Yukon and south to the mountains of New England but it does not occur in the Arctic. A plant and an enlarged perigynium and scale are shown on p. 57, d.

(21) **Few-flowered Sedge** *Carex rariflora* (Wahlenb.) Sm. This and the two following species are all rather slender with felted or hairy roots and nodding spikes borne on slender stalks. In *C. rariflora* the stalk of the staminate spike is less than $\frac{1}{2}$ inch long; the perigynia are beakless and ovoid; and the scales are about the same length and width as the perigynia, are purple-brown, and curved so that they enclose the perigynia. The species is circumboreal in the Arctic and extends south, in cold bogs, to Newfoundland and eastern Quebec. It is a very rare sedge in our area, being known only from Katahdin. A plant and an enlarged perigynium and scale are shown on p. 59, a.

(22) **Quagmire Sedge** *Carex limosa* L. The quagmire sedge differs from the previous species in having the stalk of the staminate spike more than $\frac{1}{2}$ inch long; and the scales not enclosing the perigynia. It is another circumboreal species which extends south to Pennsylvania and California. It is occasional in lowland bogs of our area and has been found in an alpine bog on Mt. Lafayette. A plant and an enlarged perigynium and scale are shown on p. 59, b.

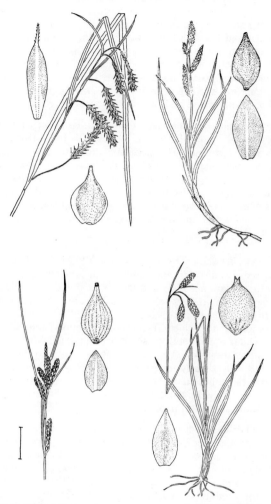

a. **Long-haired Sedge**
   Carex crinita, var. *simulans*

b. **Bigelow's Sedge**
   Carex Bigelowii

c. **White Mountain Sedge**
   Carex lenticularis, var. *albi-montana*

d. **Black Sedge**
   Carex atratiformis

(23) **Very Depauperate Sedge** *Carex paupercula* Michx. This is the most common of the three species. It is characterized by having the stalks of the staminate spikes short; the perigynia sub-orbicular; and the scales narrower and longer than the perigynia and terminating in a long slender point. The species is circumboreal in acid swamps and bogs and extends south to Pennsylvania and Colorado. Most of the collections from above treeline in our area belong to var. *irrigua* (Wahlenb.) Fern. A plant and an enlarged perigynium and scale are shown on p. 59, c.

(24) **Drooping Wood Sedge** *Carex arctata* Boott. The drooping wood sedge is a tall slender species with long slender spikes which usually droop. The perigynia are three-sided, distinctly nerved and only slightly longer than the sharp-pointed scales. The species is found in woods and thickets from Newfoundland to Ontario and south to Pennsylvania and Michigan. It is a lowland species which is occasionally found above 4000 feet in the mountains. A culm and an enlarged perigynium and scale are shown on p. 59, d.

(25) **Slender-stalked Sedge** *Carex debilis* Michx. The slender-stalked sedge is also tall and slender with long cylindrical spikes. The perigynia are nerveless and long-beaked and distinctly longer than the light-colored scales. Two varieties are found above treeline. In var. *Rudgei* Bailey the mature perigynia are brown and twice as long as the scales. This variety is found from Newfoundland to Ontario and south to North Carolina and Missouri. It is chiefly a lowland form. Var. *strictior* Bailey has the ripe perigynia green and only slightly longer than the scales. It was described from material collected on Mt. Washington and is restricted to the mountains of New England. A culm and an enlarged perigynium and scale are shown on p. 60, a.

(26) **Hair-like Sedge** *Carex capillaris* L. The hair-like sedge is a low, slender species with small, few-flowered drooping spikes. The perigynia are small, distinctly beaked, and longer than the broad, light-colored scales. It is a circumboreal arctic-alpine species which extends south to Mt. Washington, where it is very local, and to the mountains of Colorado. The relatively more robust var. *major* Blytt is somewhat more widely distributed in our area. A plant and an enlarged perigynium and scale are shown on p. 60, b.

(27) **Finely-nerved Sedge** *Carex leptonervia* Fern. The finely-nerved sedge is a fairly tall slender species with cylindrical spikes. The perigynia are spindle-shaped, the straightish beaks being about

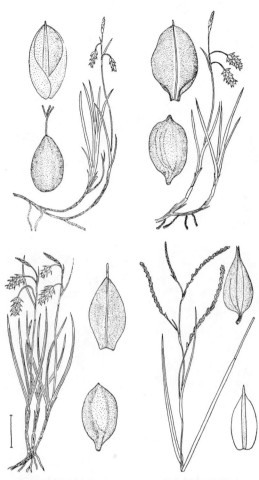

a. **Few-flowered Sedge**
   Carex rariflora

b. **Quagmire Sedge**
   Carex limosa

c. **Very Depauperate Sedge**
   Carex paupercula

d. **Drooping Wood Sedge**
   Carex arctata

as long as the stipes. In spite of the name the perigynia are nerveless or only faintly nerved. The scales are broader above than at the base and sometimes terminate in a short awn. It is a northern and upland species found in low woods from Labrador to northern

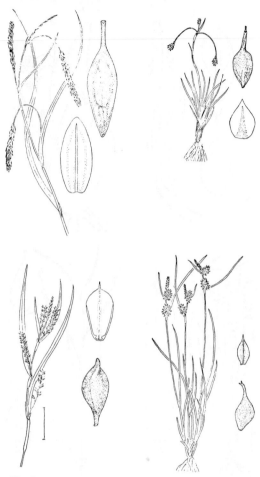

a. **Slender-stalked Sedge**
   Carex debilis

b. **Hair-like Sedge**
   Carex capillaris

c. **Finely-nerved Sedge**
   Carex leptonervia

d. **Yellowish Sedge**
   Carex flava, var. *fertilis*

Minnesota and south to North Carolina and Tennessee. It is more common at lower elevations but occasionally occurs well up on the mountains. The upper portion of a culm and an enlarged perigynium and scale are shown on p. 60, c.

(28)   **Yellowish Sedge** *Carex flava* L. *C. flava* is a sedge of moderate height with sessile or very short-stalked spikes and divergent perigynia. The perigynia are yellowish or green, ovoid, and tapering to a curved beak. The scales are lance-shaped and sharp-pointed. The species occurs in Europe and from Labrador to Alaska and south to Pennsylvania and Montana. It is a variable species. Material found on the mountains is probably var. *fertilis* Peck with greenish recurving perigynia which almost hide the pale scales. A plant and an enlarged perigynium and scale are shown on p. 60, d.

(29)   **Michaux's Sedge** *Carex Michauxiana* Boeckl. Michaux's sedge is a striking species of moderate height. The perigynia are $\frac{1}{2}$ inch long, slenderly lance-shaped and strongly divergent. The scales are less than half as long as the perigynia. The species is found in bogs in eastern Asia, and from Newfoundland to Ontario and south to Massachusetts and Michigan. While usually found at lower elevations it also occurs around Eagle Lake on Mt. Lafayette and high up on Mt. Mansfield. A plant and an enlarged perigynium and scale are shown on p. 63, a.

(30)   **Inflated Sedge** *Carex intumescens* Rudge. The spreading perigynia of this species are much inflated and over half as broad as long. The scales are much narrower and shorter than the perigynia. It is one of the common species of swamps and swales throughout the East at moderate elevations. It has been found on the Fan in Huntington Ravine on Mt. Washington and at 5000 feet on Mt. Marcy. A culm and an enlarged perigynium and scale are shown on p. 63, b.

(31)   **Beaked Sedge** *Carex rostrata* Stokes. The beaked sedge is a stout tall species with relatively broad leaves and cylindric many-flowered spikes. The perigynia are flask-shaped, beaked and distinctly nerved. The scales are narrower and shorter than the perigynia. The species is circumboreal and occurs south to Tennessee and New Mexico. It usually occurs in wet ground at low elevations but it is also found around Eagle Lake on Mt. Lafayette. The upper portion of a culm and an enlarged perigynium and scale are shown on p. 63, c.

(32)   **Few-seeded Sedge** *Carex oligosperma* Michx. The few-seeded sedge is a slender species with narrower leaves and globular, few-flowered spikes. The perigynia are much inflated and half as broad as long. The scales are also broad and nearly as long as the perigynia. It is a bog species found from Labrador to the Mackenzie and south to Pennsylvania and Indiana. It seldom gets

above 3000 feet in the White Mountains but has been collected at 5000 feet on Mt. Marcy. The inflorescence and an enlarged perigynium and scale are shown on p. 63, d.

JUNCACEAE (Rush Family)

The members of this family resemble the grasses and sedges in general appearance but the structure of the flowers is entirely different. Although small, the flowers are much like those of members of the lily family with three sepals, three petals, three or six stamens, and a three-parted capsule. The capsule of *Juncus* is three-celled and many-seeded while that of *Luzula* is one-celled and three-seeded. The fruits of grasses and sedges are always one-seeded. *Juncus* is a fairly large genus but the three species treated here are easily differentiated. There are far fewer species in the genus *Luzula* although there are four in our area.

1. Flowers aggregated into dense many-flowered spikes . . . . 5.
1. Flowers not aggregated into dense spikes . . . . 2.
   2. Leaves broad and flat; inflorescence terminal, loose, open, and many flowered
                (4) Small-flowered Woodrush *Luzula parviflora*
   2. Leaves not broad . . . . 3.
3. Leaves transversely septate
           (3) Short-tailed Rush *Juncus brevicaudatus*
3. Leaves not septate . . . . 4.
   4. Densely tufted plants; inflorescence terminal with relatively few flowers   **(1) Highland Rush** *Juncus trifidus*
   4. Plants not tufted; inflorescence appearing to grow from side of stem, several flowered
                (2) Thread Rush *Juncus filiformis*
5. Leaves broad, flat, and hairy
          (7) Many-flowered Woodrush *Luzula multiflora*
5. Leaves not broad and flat . . . . 6.
   6. Spikes oval, on erect peduncles
           (6) Northern Woodrush *Luzula confusa*
   6. Spikes elongate, nodding
           (5) Spiked Woodrush *Luzula spicata*

(1)   **Highland Rush** *Juncus trifidus* L. The highland rush is a true arctic-alpine plant. Above treeline its dense tufts of relatively short stems are one of the principal constituents of such turf as is present. The plants are usually less than a foot tall, the stems bear few leaves, and the small and inconspicuous flowers are lo-

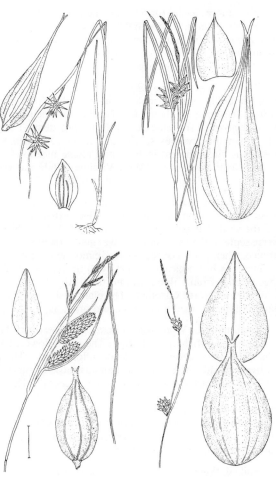

a. **Michaux's Sedge**
   Carex Michauxiana

b. **Inflated Sedge**
   Carex intumescens

c. **Beaked Sedge**
   Carex rostrata

d. **Few-seeded Sedge**
   Carex oligosperma

cated in a cluster of two or three leaves at the top of the stem.
The species is found from Greenland, where it grows well north of
the Arctic Circle, to the high mountains of our area and in similar
habitats in Europe and Asia. Var. *monanthos* (Jacq.) Bluff &

Fingerhuth, a more slender form with numerous basal leaves which are as long as the stems, is occasionally found at lower elevations in our area and on the mountains of Virginia and North Carolina as well as in Europe. (Three-forked rush.) The plant is shown on Pl. 8, 1; the plant and an enlarged flower on p. 65, a.

(2)   **Thread Rush** *Juncus filiformis* L. The thread rush is a common plant of bogs at lower elevations but is less frequent above timberline. It belongs to the group of rushes in which the flowers appear to be growing from the side of the leafless stem. The plants are taller than the previous species and never form dense tufts. The species is circumboreal in bogs and alpine meadows; it extends south to the uplands of West Virginia, Utah and Oregon. The plant and an enlarged flower are shown on p. 65, b.

(3)   **Short-tailed Rush** *Juncus brevicaudatus* (Engelm.) Fern. This rush gets its name from the appendages extending from the ends of the seeds. It belongs to the group of rushes which have transverse septa in the tissue of the leaves giving them a corrugated appearance, when dry. The species is common in muddy places at lower elevations but occasionally gets well up on the mountains. Its range extends from Labrador to northern Alberta and south to the mountains of North Carolina. The plant is shown on Pl. 8, 2; the plant and an enlarged flower and seed on p. 69, a.

(4)   **Small-flowered Woodrush** *Luzula parviflora* (Ehrh.) Desv., var. *melanocarpa* (Michx.) Buchenau. The small-flowered wood-rush has the flowers scattered in a loose inflorescence. The leaves are relatively broad and are not so hairy as those of most wood-rushes. The plants are sometimes more than 2 feet tall. The species is common in our area in rich woods and along alpine brooks. It is circumboreal in its distribution; in North America it occurs from Labrador to Alaska and southward to our area and to the mountains of Arizona. The inflorescence is shown on Pl. 8, 3; the plant and an enlarged flower on p. 65, c.

(5)   **Spiked Woodrush** *Luzula spicata* (L.) DC. The spiked woodrush bears its flowers in nodding brown spikes which when seen singly are not particularly attractive, but in a mass are truly beautiful. The leaves are narrow and channeled. It is an arctic-alpine plant with a circumboreal distribution very similar to that of the previous species. The plant and an enlarged flower are shown on p. 65, d.

(6)   **Northern Woodrush** *Luzula confusa* Lindeberg. The north-ern woodrush is only half as tall as the previous species. The

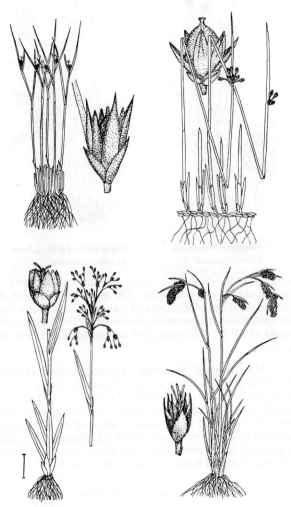

a. **Highland Rush**
   Juncus trifidus

b. **Thread Rush**
   Juncus filiformis

c. **Small-flowered Woodrush**
   Luzula parviflora, var. *melanocarpa*

d. **Spiked Woodrush**
   Luzula spicata

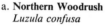

a. **Northern Woodrush**
Luzula confusa

b. **Many-flowered Woodrush**
Luzula multiflora

flowers are borne in a dense, erect, chestnut-brown spike. The leaves are narrow and channeled. The plants form tufts in alpine regions of the White Mountains and Katahdin. It is another arctic-alpine species with a circumpolar distribution. On Ellesmere Island it occurs at 83° N. The plant and an enlarged flower are shown on p. 66, a.

(7)   **Many-flowered Woodrush**   *Luzula multiflora* (Retz.) Lejeune. This is the common *Luzula* of our area being a lowland plant of meadows and open woods. The leaves are broad, flat, and distinctly hairy. The spikes are usually erect and pale- or reddish-brown. It is common in the cooler regions of both hemispheres. It has been collected on the summit of Mt. Washington and probably gets well up on other mountains of our area. The plant and an enlarged bud and flower are shown on p. 66, b.

LILIACEAE (Lily Family)

The members of the lily family are typical Monocotyledons. With the exception of *Maianthemum* the flowers are built on a basic plan of three, three sepals, three petals, six stamens, and a three-parted pistil. In most of the species the sepals and petals are very much alike and are jointly called perianth segments. Except for *Veratrum*

66

the fruits of the species here treated are berries. None of the species has a woody stem, in fact the only Monocotyledon of our area which is woody is the greenbrier. The principal veins of the leaves are parallel with the exception of *Trillium*. The members of this family make up a fairly conspicuous part of our spring flora and the family is well represented above treeline.

1. Sepals and petals much alike . . . . 2.
1. Sepals three, green; petals three, white except for purple lines
   at base; leaves three, in a whorl at top of stem
   (9) Painted Trillium   *Trillium undulatum*
2. Flowers bell-shaped and nodding . . . . 6.
2. Flowers neither bell-shaped nor nodding . . . . 3.
3. Stem stout, 2–6 feet tall; leaves broad and numerous; flowers
   yellow-green, borne in a pyramidal inflorescence
   (1) Indian Poke   *Veratrum viride*
3. Plants slender, less than 2 feet tall; flowers white . . . . . 4.
4. Flowers of six petal-like parts; stem with three or more
   leaves which taper to both ends . . . . 5.
4. Flowers of four petal-like parts; stem with usually two
   leaves which are broadest at base
   (5) Canada Mayflower   *Maianthemum canadense*
5. Tall plants; leaves numerous; flowers many
   (3) False Spikenard   *Smilacina racemosa*
5. Shorter plants; leaves usually three; flowers three to eight
   (4) Three-leaved False Solomon's-seal   *Smilacina trifolia*
6. Leaves all basal; flowers yellow-green; berries blue
   (2) Clintonia   *Clintonia borealis*
6. Stems leafy, branched; berries red . . . . 7.
7. Plants not hairy; leaves strongly clasping; flowers greenish-
   white
   (6) Clasping-leaved Twisted-stalk   *Streptopus amplexifolius*
7. Plants hairy; flowers reddish or purplish . . . . 8.
8. Leaves not clasping; flowers pink or rose-purple
   (8) Sessile-leaved Twisted-stalk   *Streptopus roseus*
8. Leaves clasping; flowers roseate to deep purple
   (7) Hybrid Twisted-stalk   X *Streptopus oreopolus*

(1)   **Indian Poke**   *Veratrum viride* Ait. The spikes of the Indian poke start developing almost as soon as the snow melts, and when young they look somewhat like heads of Chinese cabbage. They develop into a stalk about a yard tall bearing broad, strongly-veined leaves and terminating in a large spike of yellowish-green flowers. The plant is common in cool swamps across North America and is fairly abundant in wet places above timberline. When eaten it

acts as a powerful and violent narcotic. A drug used in the treatment of high blood pressure is obtained from the roots and base of the stem. (False hellebore, white hellebore, itchweed.) The inflorescence and some of the upper leaves are shown on Pl. 8, 4.

(2)   **Clintonia**   *Clintonia borealis* (Ait.) Raf. The genus was named by Rafinesque in honor of DeWitt Clinton, one-time governor of New York. The large basal leaves of clintonia look somewhat like those of our lady's slipper, but they are more shiny and less hairy than the latter. The scape bears several lily-like yellow-green flowers at its summit. The fruits are large, deep blue berries, more attractive than the flowers and the source of the common name "bluebead-lily." The plant is found in cool woods from Georgia to Labrador and west to Minnesota and Manitoba. Clintonia is common in and near the krummholz in alpine areas. (Corn-lily, straw-lily, cow-tongue.) The inflorescence and a portion of a leaf are shown on Pl. 9, 3.

(3)   **False Spikenard**   *Smilacina racemosa* (L.) Desf. The false spikenard has a fairly tall arching stem bearing a number of alternate leaves which taper to each end. The stem terminates in an inflorescence containing a large number of small blossoms. The fruits are small red berries. The species is found in woods and clearings from Quebec to British Columbia and south to the uplands of North Carolina and Tennessee. While it is not found above treeline it does ascend up to at least 4000 feet on the mountains. (False Solomon's-seal, Solomon's zigzag, scurvy-berries.) The plant is seen on Pl. 11, 2.

(4)   **Three-leaved False Solomon's-seal**   *Smilacina trifolia* (L.) Desf. This species is a much smaller plant which, as the name implies, usually has only three leaves on the stem. At the top of the stem are three to eight flowers which are larger and more conspicuous than those of the previous species. This species is found in bogs and wet mossy woods in Siberia, and from Labrador to the Mackenzie and south to Pennsylvania. It has been found above treeline about Star Lake on Mt. Madison and is to be looked for in similar habitats on other mountains. A plant with developing fruits is shown on Pl. 9, 2.

(5)   **Canada Mayflower**   *Maianthemum canadense* Desf. This plant is much commoner than the previous species. It is shorter and the stem usually bears two oval or somewhat heart-shaped leaves and a spike of small white flowers. The four-parted arrangement of the flowers is unusual for a Monocotyledon. The generic

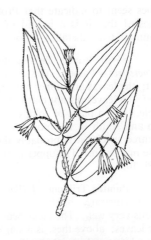

a. Short-tailed Rush
Juncus brevicaudatus

b. Hybrid Twisted-stalk
X *Streptopus oreopolus*

name means mayflower. The species is found in damp woods from Labrador to Manitoba and south to Georgia and Iowa. It is frequently found above the trees in alpine regions. (False lily of the valley, two-leaved false Solomon's-seal, beadruby, scurvy-berries.) The plant is seen on Pl. 9, 1.

(6)   **Clasping-leaved Twisted-stalk** *Streptopus amplexifolius* (L.) DC., var. *americanus* Schultes. There are three twisted-stalks in our area. This species, which is sometimes called liverberry, is relatively large; the leaves are smooth and clasp the stem; the flowers are greenish-white. The variety is found in eastern Asia, from Greenland to Manitoba and south to North Carolina, and from Alaska to New Mexico. In our area it is occasionally found above treeline. (Liverberry, scootberry, white mandarin.) A plant with fruits is shown on Pl. 10, 2.

(7)   **Hybrid Twisted-stalk** X *Streptopus oreopolus* Fern. The hybrid twisted-stalk is the least common of the three species and combines the characters of the other two. It is a large plant; the leaves are clasping as in *S. amplexifolius* but hairy as in *S. roseus*; the flowers are rose-colored to deep purple; the berries apparently never contain viable seed. The species is known from Newfoundland, the Mingan Islands, the Shickshock Mountains, Katahdin and Mt. Washington. The true position of this plant has been a matter of discussion for the past fifty years. Recent cytological

studies seem to indicate that Prof. Fernald was correct when he suggested that it is a hybrid of *S. amplexifolius* and *S. roseus*. (Mountain twisted-stalk.) A portion of the plant is seen on p. 69, b.

(8)   **Sessile-leaved Twisted-stalk** *Streptopus roseus* Michx., var. *perspectus* Fassett. The sessile-leaved twisted-stalk is a smaller plant; the leaves and upper part of the stem are covered with short hairs; the leaves do not clasp the stem; and the flowers are rose-purple. It is a plant of cold, damp woods from Labrador to Ontario and south to the mountains of Georgia and Kentucky. Of the three species it is probably the most common above treeline. (Rose mandarin.) The upper part of the stem, with flowers, is seen on Pl. 10, 1.

(9)   **Painted Trillium** *Trillium undulatum* Willd. The painted trillium illustrates the three-parted arrangement of the Monocotyledons very well. The stem bears at its summit a whorl of three large leaves; above these is a single flower with three green sepals, three white petals painted with purple veins at the bases, six stamens, and a three-parted pistil. The species is found in cold damp woods from Quebec to the mountains of Georgia and westward to Manitoba and Wisconsin. It is common in the woods at lower elevations and occasional well up on the mountains. The three summit leaves, sepals and petals are seen on Pl. 9, 4.

ORCHIDACEAE (Orchis Family)

The orchis family and the composite family are the largest families of flowering plants, each containing between 15,000 and 20,000 species. Most of the orchids grow in the warmer parts of the world and only three species are likely to be found above timberline in our area; none of the three is very showy. The orchid flower is very specialized and highly modified for insect pollination. There are three sepals, the upper one being larger than the lateral ones. There are also three petals, the lower petal is modified into the lip. There is a single functional stamen. The pollen grains are compacted into structures known as pollinia and occasionally one may see a male mosquito flying about bearing a pollinium on its head.

1. Leaf solitary and basal
                      (2) **Blunt-leaf Orchid**   *Habenaria obtusata*
1. Stem with two to several leaves . . . . 2.
    2. Stem with several lance-shaped leaves, alternately arranged
                   (1) **Tall Leafy White Orchid**   *Habenaria dilatata*

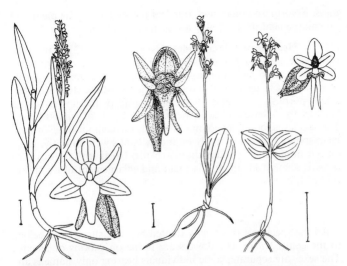

a. **Tall Leafy White
Orchid**
Habenaria dilatata

b. **Blunt-leaf Orchid**
*Habenaria
obtusata*

c. **Heart-leaved Twayblade**
Listera cordata

2. Stem with two opposite ovate leaves
         (3) **Heart-leaved Twayblade** *Listera cordata*

(1)   **Tall Leafy White Orchid** *Habenaria dilatata* (Pursh)
Hook. This is the largest and most abundant of the three orchids
here described. The stems are leafy and often nearly 2 feet tall. At
the summit of the stem is a spike of many small white blossoms.
This species is found in bogs and wet woods across the continent
from Labrador to Alaska and southward to Pennsylvania in the
East and California in the West. It is fairly frequent on moist alpine
banks such as the headwall of Tuckerman Ravine on Mt. Washington. (Fragrant white orchid, white-lance, bog-candle, lozenge-
lip, scent-bottle.) The inflorescence is seen on Pl. 10, 3; the plant
and an enlarged flower on p. 71, a.

(2)   **Blunt-leaf Orchid** *Habenaria obtusata* (Pursh) Richards.
The stem of this plant is usually less than 10 inches tall and the
only leaf is basal. The flowers are relatively few in number and
greenish-white. It is a plant of mossy coniferous woods from Labrador to Alaska and southward to Massachusetts and New York
in the East and Colorado in the West. While usually found at lower
elevations it may occur in the evergreen forest well up on the moun-

71

tains. (Northern bog-orchid, one-leaf rein-orchid.) The plant and an enlargement of the flower are seen on p. 71, b.

(3)   **Heart-leaved Twayblade**   *Listera cordata* (L.) R.Br. The twayblade is so small and unassuming that it is easily overlooked. The stems are 6 inches or less tall and bear about midway a pair of somewhat heart-shaped leaves. At the top of the stem are a few small, purplish to greenish flowers. The lip of the flower is split halfway to its base and near the base are a pair of curved horns. The species is found in cool mossy woods throughout the Northern Hemisphere and occasionally on mossy banks well up in the scrub on our mountains. (Mannikin twayblade, Northern Listera.) The plant is seen on Pl. 10, 4; the plant and enlargement of the flower on p. 71, c.

SALICACEAE (Willow Family)

All the species of this family treated here are shrubs and belong to the genus *Salix*. The flowers are borne on catkins or aments. The sexes are separate, some individuals bearing only stamens and other individuals only pistils. The catkins of the two sexes look much alike when young and in the pussy willow stage. As they mature the male aments become covered with yellow pollen; the aments fall after the pollen has been discharged. As the female or fertile aments mature the pistils become modified into capsules containing many small seeds covered with a silky down. The capsules finally split allowing the seeds to blow away. In collecting willows for study, specimens bearing mature fertile aments are the most useful and only female aments or capsules are shown in the drawings.

Identification of willows is not easy. It is sometimes difficult to match the male and female plants of the same species. A more perplexing situation is frequently encountered due to the ease with which the various species hybridize, the hybrids showing various combinations of the characters of the two parent species. Fortunately, comparatively few willows occur above treeline.

1. Fruit smooth . . . . 2.
1. Fruit covered with short hairs . . . . 6.
  2. Erect shrubs . . . . 3.
  2. Prostrate or creeping alpine shrubs . . . . 4.
3. Leaves long and narrow with conspicuous stipules at the base
                            (7) **Stiff Willow**   *Salix rigida*
3. Leaves broadly rounded at the base, stipules absent
                            (6) **Balsam Willow**   *Salix pyrifolia*

4. Leaves at least twice as long as broad, narrowed to the base, at most only slightly toothed

                       (3) **Bearberry Willow** *Salix Uva-ursi*

4. Leaves less than twice as long as broad, distinctly toothed 5.

5. Leaves narrowing to the base; fertile catkins with at least twenty fruits   (2) **Pease's Willow** X *Salix Peasei*

5. Leaves roundish; fertile catkins usually with fewer than ten fruits   (1) **Dwarf Willow** *Salix herbacea*

   6. Leaves smooth on both surfaces . . . . 7.

   6. Leaves hairy, at least beneath . . . . 9.

7. Prostrate shrubs with short broad leaves

               (4) **Arctic-loving Willow** *Salix arctophila*

7. Erect or sprawling shrubs; leaves longer and narrower . . 8.

   8. Leaves with small but distinct teeth, stipules large and conspicuous   (9) **Glaucous Willow** *Salix discolor*

   8. Leaves very obscurely toothed, smooth and shining, stipules absent   (11) **Tea-leaved Willow** *Salix planifolia*

9. More than 3 feet tall . . . . 10.

9. Less than 2 feet tall; leaves and fruit with silky hairs

               (5) **Silver Willow** *Salix argyrocarpa*

   10. Leaves white and woolly beneath; stalk of fruit little longer than the scale   (10) **Prairie Willow** *Salix humilis*

   10. Leaves green with scattered down beneath; stalk of fruit much longer than the scale

             (8) **Long-beaked Willow** *Salix Bebbiana*

(1)   **Dwarf Willow** *Salix herbacea* L. The dwarf willow is the smallest of our willows with the visible portions only a few inches long. The leaves are broadly oval to somewhat heart-shaped with rounded teeth on the margin, and green on both faces. The mature catkins are small with few capsules. The dwarf willow extends north of the Arctic Circle in Europe, Asia and North America. Its southern limit on this continent is Katahdin, the White Mountains and the Adirondacks; it is not found in western America. It is usually much less common in our area than the bearberry willow. The plant is shown on Pl. 11, 1.

(2)   **Pease's Willow** X *Salix Peasei* Fern. This willow is named for Prof. A. S. Pease who discovered it in King Ravine on Mt. Adams. It is presumably a hybrid of the dwarf willow and the bearberry willow. It has the spreading habit of the bearberry willow and the leaves have a tendency to taper to the base, but in most respects it more closely resembles the dwarf willow although the fertile catkins are larger and contain more capsules. It is known

only from the type station and two stations west of Hudson Bay. A portion of a plant and an enlarged capsule are seen on p. 75, a.

(3)   **Bearberry Willow**   *Salix Uva-ursi* Pursh. The bearberry willow is a dwarf prostrate plant of the Arctic and alpine summits. The name is derived from the resemblance of the leaves to those of the bearberry. The leaves are elliptical, tapering to the base, deep green above and paler beneath. The fertile catkins are usually about an inch long with smooth brown capsules. Its range is from Greenland to Baffin Island and south to the mountains of our area. Pl. 11, 3 shows a female plant and 11, 4 a male plant.

(4)   **Arctic-loving Willow**   *Salix arctophila* Cockerell. This is another dwarf arctic willow with a prostrate stem. The leaves are short and broader above the midpoint than below. The fertile capsules are large, sometimes reaching a length of nearly 4 inches. The capsules are also large and pubescent, at least when young. It is common on the arctic tundra and occurs on alpine barrens as far south as Katahdin where it is known from one very limited area. A portion of the plant and an enlarged capsule are seen on p. 75, b.

(5)   **Silver Willow**   *Salix argyrocarpa* Anderss. The silver willow has narrow elliptical leaves which are deep green above and covered with silky white hairs beneath; the stipules are small and soon lost. The fruiting catkins are about an inch long; the capsules are covered with silvery, silky hairs. The shrub is seldom more than a foot and a half tall; the twigs are deep olive green. The silver willow is found from Labrador to the high mountains of Quebec, Maine and New Hampshire. Staminate plants are said to be rare. A portion of the plant and an enlarged capsule are seen on p. 75, c.

A hybrid of this species and *S. planifolia* was collected by Asa Gray in Tuckerman Ravine in 1842. It is known as X *S. Grayi* Schneid. and is occasionally found on Mt. Washington.

(6)   **Balsam Willow**   *Salix pyrifolia* Anderss. This is a common shrub of low ground which is sometimes found close to timberline. The twigs are often a tan red. The leaves are broad for a willow and frequently somewhat heart-shaped; the underside is much paler than the upper, and the veins are prominent. Stipules are minute or lacking. The mature fertile catkins may be 3 inches long and loose and drooping; the capsules are smooth and slender with long stalks. The species is found from Labrador to British Columbia and southward to northern New England, New York and Minnesota. A leaf and an enlarged capsule are seen on p. 75, d.

74

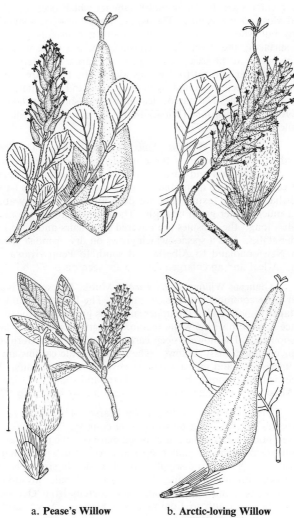

a. **Pease's Willow**
   X *Salix Peasei*

b. **Arctic-loving Willow**
   Salix arctophila

c. **Silver Willow**
   Salix argyrocarpa

d. **Balsam Willow**
   Salix pyrifolia

(7)   **Stiff Willow** *Salix rigida* Muhl. The stiff willow is another common shrub of low moist habitats which occasionally is found close to timberline. The young leaves may be somewhat downy but when mature they are smooth and usually green on both surfaces; the shape varies considerably and there may be a shallow notch at the base. The stipules are large. The fertile catkins are slender and up to 2 inches long. The twigs are yellow-green. This species is found from Newfoundland to Ontario and south to Georgia. The narrow-leafed extreme shown in the illustration is var. *angustata* (Pursh) Fern. A leaf and an enlarged capsule are seen on p. 77, a.

(8)   **Long-beaked Willow** *Salix Bebbiana* Sarg. The long-beaked willow is another of those wanderers from lower ground. It is a very common and variable species. The leaves are usually elliptical and toothed along the margin; the mature leaves have a somewhat leathery texture and are deep green and downy above and a much lighter green beneath. The mature catkins are about 3 inches long; the capsules are covered with hairs and have long slender stalks. It is a species which grows on dry or moist ground from Newfoundland to Alberta and south to Pennsylvania and Iowa. A leaf and an enlarged capsule are seen on p. 77, b.

(9)   **Glaucous Willow** *Salix discolor* Muhl. This species is also much more common at lower elevations. The leaves are elliptical and taper to both ends; the upper surface is green while the under surface is smooth with a white bloom. The stipules are fairly large but soon fall. The flowers open early in the spring and form one of our common pussy willows. The mature fertile catkins are up to 3 inches long and the capsules are covered with soft hairs. The species is found from Labrador to Alberta and south to Delaware and Missouri. A leaf and an enlarged capsule are seen on p. 77, c.

(10)   **Prairie Willow** *Salix humilis* Marsh. This is the last of the species which wander up from lower country. The leaves tend to be elliptical with toothed or crinkled margins; the upper surface is dull green while the under surface is covered with a mat of grayish-white hairs. The stipules are of moderate size. The mature catkins are about an inch long and the capsules are downy. This shrub is found on dry plains and barrens from Quebec to Minnesota and south to Louisiana and Kansas. A leaf and an enlarged capsule are seen on p. 77, d.

(11)   **Tea-leaved Willow** *Salix planifolia* Pursh. The tea-leaved willow has elliptic-lanceolate leaves which are smooth and somewhat leathery in texture; the upper surface is lustrous green and

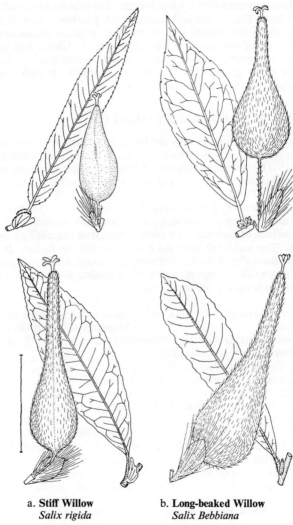

a. **Stiff Willow**
Salix rigida

b. **Long-beaked Willow**
Salix Bebbiana

c. **Glaucous Willow**
Salix discolor

d. **Prairie Willow**
Salix humilis

the lower covered with a white bloom. The stipules are small and soon lost. The mature catkins are about 2 inches long with capsules which are covered with hairs. The twigs are plum-colored. The range of the species is from Labrador to Alberta and south to the mountains of New England. A very similar species is found in the cooler parts of the Old World. A fruiting branch and an enlarged capsule are seen on p. 79, a.

CORYLACEAE (Hazel Family)

In this family the flowers are borne in aments which are either male or female but both kinds of aments are carried by the same plant. The staminate catkins are long and slender, mature early in the growing season, and fall soon after the pollen has been discharged. The family includes the birches and the alders. The female aments of the birches are shorter and broader than the male and are made up of thin scales which are three-parted at the tip. At the base of each scale is a small winged fruit containing a single seed. The scales fall after the fruits have left the catkin. In the alders the scales of the fertile aments are stouter and woody, forming a cone-like structure which often persists over winter. The fruits are winged as in the birches.

1. Fertile catkins with thick woody scales which persist over winter   (5) **Mountain Alder**   *Alnus crispa*
1. Fertile catkins with thin three-lobed scales which fall soon after the winged nutlets fall . . . . 2.
  2. Young twigs fuzzy or hairy . . . . 3.
  2. Young twigs glabrous, often glutinous . . . . 4.
3. Leaves triangular in outline, slightly notched at base
    (2) **Heart-leaved Paper Birch**   *Betula papyrifera*, var. *cordifolia*
3. Leaves elliptical to obovate, often tapering to base
                  (3) **Northern Birch**   *Betula borealis*
  4. Leaves longer than broad; wings of fruit broader than nutlets   (1) **Small Birch**   *Betula minor*
  4. Leaves about as broad as long; wings of fruit narrower than nutlets   (4) **Dwarf Birch**   *Betula glandulosa*

(1)   **Small Birch**   *Betula minor* (Tuckerm.) Fern. The small birch is a shrub of the subarctic and the mountains. The twigs are gummy but never fuzzy. The leaves are of moderate size and rounded or tapered to the base. This birch is found on barrens and alpine summits from Labrador to the mountains of New England and New York. The type on which the species is based was

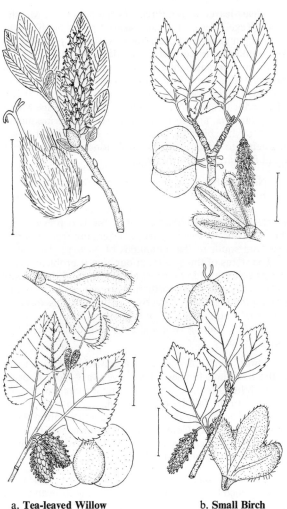

a. **Tea-leaved Willow**
   Salix planifolia

b. **Small Birch**
   Betula minor

c. **Heart-leaved Paper Birch**
   Betula papyrifera, var. *cordifolia*

d. **Northern Birch**
   Betula borealis

collected by Tuckerman in the White Mountains. A fruiting branch and an enlarged scale and fruit are seen on p. 79, b.

(2)   **Heart-leaved Paper Birch** *Betula papyrifera* Marsh., var. *cordifolia* (Regel) Fern. The heart-leaved paper birch is a variety of the common paper birch. At low elevations it is a large tree but on the mountains it is reduced to a moderate-sized shrub. It differs from the common paper birch in having a heart-shaped notch at the base of the leaf and in having somewhat larger scales on the fertile catkins. The young twigs are somewhat fuzzy. It is found from Labrador to Ontario and south to the Blue Ridge Mountains in North Carolina, and to northern Iowa. In the mountains it is the common white birch of northern New England and New York and it extends to high elevations. A fruiting twig and an enlarged scale and fruit are seen on p. 79, c.

(3)   **Northern Birch** *Betula borealis* Spach. The northern birch is a shrub with decidedly hairy young twigs. The leaves are ovate or elliptic and longer than broad. The scales of the fertile catkins are shorter and broader than those of the two previous species. The range of the species is given as extending from Labrador to Ungava, and south to the mountains of New England and New York. The status of this species in our area is problematical. The number of collections in herbaria are few and, of the collections I have seen, only one from northern Vermont, and apparently not from an alpine area, seems clearly to belong to this species. Any collections of mature material of this species from our area would be welcome. A fruiting twig and an enlarged scale and fruit are seen on p. 79, d.

(4)   **Dwarf Birch** *Betula glandulosa* Michx. This is the smallest of the mountain birches. The leaves vary from obovate and over an inch long to kidney-shaped or almost circular and scarcely $\frac{1}{4}$ inch long. In the fall the leaves become a rich copper-red. The species occurs across the American Arctic and south in the mountains to New England, Colorado and California. It is present on Katahdin, the Presidentials and Mt. Marcy. Autumn foliage and winter buds are seen on Pl. 12, 4.

(5)   **Mountain Alder** *Alnus crispa* (Ait.) Pursh. The mountain alder looks much like the common alders found in swamps at lower elevations but the leaves and flowers appear at the same time while in the latter species the flowers appear much earlier than the leaves. The typical variety, which is the commoner one on the mountains, is nearly glabrous. Var. *mollis* Fern., which is more frequent at lower elevations, has the twigs and under surfaces of the leaves pubescent. The species is found from Labrador to Alberta and south to the mountains of North Carolina and Wisconsin. It is

frequent on all our mountains. Foliage and aments are seen on Pl. 12, 3.

SANTALACEAE (Sandalwood Family)

The sandalwood family is a small family of plants which are mostly tropical in their distribution and many of the species are parasitic on the roots of other seed plants. Only two species occur in our area. The bastard-toadflax, *Comandra umbellata*, is found in the lowlands and *Geocaulon* on the mountains. Both have somewhat woody creeping rootstocks which send up herbaceous stems bearing entire leaves and the flowers.

Northern Comandra *Geocaulon lividum* (Richards.) Fern. The northern comandra is easily overlooked except when it is in fruit. The herbaceous flowering stems arise from a creeping rootstock and are usually less than a foot tall. The untoothed leaves are alternate on the stem and clusters of two to four inconspicuous flowers are borne in the axils of the leaves in the midportion of the stem. One flower of each cluster is perfect and the others are staminate. The perfect flower matures into a scarlet, berry-like false drupe. The species is found in moss and damp humus from Labrador to Alaska and south to New England, New York and northern Michigan. It is not a true alpine, being more common near the summits of secondary mountains, but it can be found around the margins of the tableland of Katahdin and on the summit ridge of Mt. Mansfield. A stem with fruit is seen on p. 84, a.

POLYGONACEAE (Buckwheat Family)

This family is well represented in our lowlands, chiefly by weeds such as the docks, the sheep-sorrel, and the knotweeds or smartweeds. All our species are herbs with alternate leaves. The stems are jointed and the joints are sheathed by the stipules of the leaves, the sheathing stipules being known as *ochreae*. The flowers have sepals but no petals and the fruits are achenes. Only two species are found on our mountains.

1. Leaves broad and kidney-shaped, with a notch at the base
        (1) **Mountain Sorrel** *Oxyria digyna*
1. Leaves lance-shaped with no notch at the base
        (2) **Alpine Bistort** *Polygonum viviparum*

(1)   **Mountain Sorrel** *Oxyria digyna* (L.) Hill. The mountain sorrel is easily identified by its kidney-shaped leaves and its flowers

and fruits which resemble those of the lowland docks and sheep sorrel. It prefers damp habitats such as the small brooks in Tuckerman Ravine. In the Arctic, it is known as "scurvy-grass" as it is one of the few available green vegetables. Some Indian and Eskimo tribes gather and ferment it to form a sauerkraut which they store for winter use. The species is found throughout the Arctic; it extends south to the Presidential Range in the East and in the mountains to New Mexico and California in the West. Foliage and flowers are seen on Pl. 12, 1.

(2) **Alpine Bistort** *Polygonum viviparum* L. The alpine bistort is a low plant with a spike of flesh-colored flowers which are often modified into red bulblets. The leaves are lance-shaped, and the rootstocks are tuberous. It apparently never sets seed but is spread by the bulblets. The tubers and bulblets are regularly eaten in the North and are said to have an almond-like flavor. In spite of its being propagated only vegetatively, it is a wide-ranging species, being found throughout the Arctic, south to New Mexico along the Rocky Mountains and to the New England mountains. The inflorescence with bulblets is seen on Pl. 12, 2; the entire plant on p. 84, b.

PORTULACACEAE (Purslane Family)

This family is poorly represented in our area even in the lowlands, the only common species being the purslane, *Portulaca oleracea*, a garden weed. The plants are soft and rather watery, the leaves are entire, the flowers have a pair of sepals and a number of so-called petals which are sometimes fairly showy. A number of rather beautiful members of this family are common in the mountains of the West.

Spring Beauty *Claytonia caroliniana* Michx. The spring beauty seems a fragile plant to be blooming above treeline in June but may occasionally be found high up on the headwalls of ravines. The genus was named in honor of Dr. James Clayton, one of the early American botanists. Where abundant, the corms are sometimes gathered, boiled and eaten, the flavor resembling boiled chestnuts. The young plants may also be used as potherbs, but it seems a shameful way to treat them. The species grows in rich woods and on open slopes from Newfoundland to Saskatchewan and south to North Carolina and Minnesota. The flowers are seen on Pl. 11, 6; the entire plant on p. 84, c.

CARYOPHYLLACEAE (Pink Family)

The pink family is a large family of plants in temperate regions whose blossoms run the whole gamut from petal-less small inconspicuous flowers to very showy species with well-developed petals. The leaves are usually entire and opposite. In the lowlands of our area we have a considerable number of species, some native and many introduced weeds. On the mountains, while we have a few species, we do not have the number found on the western mountains.

1. Petals evident . . . . 3.
1. Petals shorter than the sepals or lacking . . . . 2.
   2. Stocky low plants; the stems bearing silvery scales at the leaf bases; flowers in dense terminal clusters and hidden by silvery scales   (1) **Whitlow-wort** *Paronychia argyrocoma*
   2. Slender plants without silvery scales; some flowers borne on slender stalks from leaf axils
            (4) **Northern Stitchwort** *Stellaria calycantha*
3. Flowers opening in summer; petals white or pale lavender . 4.
3. Flowers present in late spring; petals pink to lavender; low moss-like plants   (5) **Moss Campion** *Silene acaulis*
   4. Plants with numerous slender erect stems forming moss-like tufts; flowering stems bearing several flowers; common
           (2) **Mountain Sandwort** *Arenaria groenlandica*
   4. Plants with sprawling, somewhat woody stems covered with remains of old leaves; flowering stems usually one-flowered; rare (3) **Northern Sandwort** *Arenaria marcescens*

(1)   **Whitlow-wort** *Paronychia argyrocoma* (Michx.) Nutt., var. *albimontana* Fern. Both the common and scientific names of this plant refer to the similarity of the silvery scales to hangnails, the common name dating back to the sixteenth century. The whitlow-wort is not a true alpine but may be found on the bare ledges of the lower mountains. The species is found in the southern mountains from Georgia to West Virginia. The variety occurs on the mountains of western Maine and the New Hampshire mountains, with the exception of an isolated lowland station on an island in the Merrimack River near Newburyport, Massachusetts. (Silverling.) The plant is seen on Pl. 11, 5 and on p. 84, d.

(2)   **Mountain Sandwort** *Arenaria groenlandica* (Retz.) Spreng. The mountain sandwort is one of the most conspicuous plants above treeline during the summer. Its attractive white blossoms are everywhere, and the plants seem to be particularly numerous

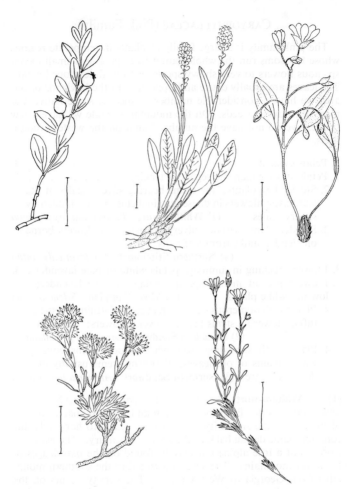

a. **Northern Comandra** b. **Alpine Bistort**   c. **Spring Beauty**
   Geocaulon lividum   *Polygonum viviparum*   *Claytonia caroliniana*

d. **Whitlow-wort**   e. **Northern Sandwort**
   Paronychia argyrocoma, var. *albimontana*   *Arenaria marcescens*

in or close to the trails so that in a thick fog the white streaks made
by the masses of blossoms are sometimes easier to follow than the
cairns. This species is confined to Greenland and Labrador south
to the mountains of New England and New York. It is also found

along the seacoast in Nova Scotia and eastern Maine. A variety continues southward, often at lower elevations, to Georgia. The plant is seen on Pl. 13, 1; 32, 1.

(3) **Northern Sandwort** *Arenaria marcescens* Fern. This species should probably not have been included in this book since in our area it has been found at only one sub-alpine station in Vermont, but it is here in the hope someone may find another station. The stems are somewhat woody and sprawling, and are covered by the remnants of the old leaves. The leaves are thick-ribbed and round-tipped. The sepals also have a conspicuous rib. The flowers are usually borne singly. In addition to the Vermont station the species is known from Mt. Albert on the Gaspé Peninsula in Quebec and from western Newfoundland. The plant is seen on p. 84, e.

(4) **Northern Stitchwort** *Stellaria calycantha* (Ledeb.) Bong. The northern stitchwort is an inconspicuous chickweed with weak, much-branched stems and small flowers. It is a plant of cool rills and not strictly an alpine. The species has been divided into several varieties, most of the plants of our area belonging either to var. *calycantha* or to var. *isophylla* Fern. which has somewhat longer and narrower leaves than the typical variety. The species and its varieties are circumboreal and in the United States their range extends south to West Virginia in the East and California in the West. The plant is seen on Pl. 14, 4.

(5) **Moss Campion** *Silene acaulis* L., var. *exscapa* (All.) DC. The moss campion is a beautiful dwarfed and tufted pink characteristic of the spring flora in arctic and alpine barrens of the Northern Hemisphere. Mt. Washington is its southern limit in the East, and it is very local there. In the mountains of the West it forms extensive carpets. In Iceland the plant is said to be gathered, boiled, and eaten with butter, but its aesthetic value must be much greater than its food value. The flowers are seen on Pl. 14, 6; the entire plant on Pl. 21, 1.

Nymphaeaceae (Water-lily Family)

The water-lily is a conspicuous plant in our lowland ponds and the spatter-docks are equally common but not so showy. All the members of this family are aquatic. The rhizomes of the plants creep along the mud on the bottom and send up long-petioled leaves which float on the surface. In the spatter-dock the yellow petal-like structures are really sepals and the petals resemble stamens.

Spatter-dock *Nuphar variegatum* Engelm. The large floating leaves and yellow flowers of the spatter-dock or cow-lily are a familiar sight in bodies of shallow water at low elevations. The species is in no sense an alpine but it can occur on mountain lakes at fairly high elevations such as Eagle Lake on Mt. Lafayette. The total range of the species extends from Labrador to Alaska and south to Maryland and Nebraska. (Yellow pond-lily, bullhead-lily, water-collard.) A leaf and flower are seen on p. 87, a.

Ranunculaceae (Crowfoot Family)

The crowfoot or buttercup family is a large family with only a small representation on our mountains. In the lowlands it contains in addition to the buttercups many of our spring flowers such as hepaticas, anemones, marsh-marigold, and columbine. Petals may be present or lacking and the sepals are often petal-like. The flowers usually have many stamens and several to many pistils. The fruits may be either capsules as in the goldthread or achenes as in the meadow rue.

1. Tall plants; leaves divided into many leaflets; petals wanting
                      (1) **Tall Meadow Rue**   *Thalictrum polygamum*
1. Short plants; leaves three-parted and evergreen; sepals petal-like, petals minute but present
                      (2) **Goldthread**   *Coptis groenlandica*

(1)   **Tall Meadow Rue**   *Thalictrum polygamum* Muhl. The tall meadow rue is a wide-ranging species of wet meadows and is essentially a lowland plant but it makes its way well up into the moist alpine ravines. It has the characteristic dainty compound leaves of all members of the genus and relatively inconspicuous blossoms which are white or somewhat purplish. Some flowers bear only stamens, others only pistils. The species occurs from Newfoundland to Ontario and south to Georgia. (Muskrat-weed, king-of-the-meadow.) Male flowers are seen on Pl. 14, 1; foliage and flowers of both sexes on p. 87, c.

(2)   **Goldthread**   *Coptis groenlandica* (Oeder) Fern. Goldthread gets its common name from its long, bright yellow rootstocks which have a very bitter taste and are used in the drug trade as a bitter. The leaves are evergreen and shining and are composed of three leaflets. The flower stalks are leafless and usually bear a single flower with five to seven conspicuous petal-like white sepals and a corresponding number of minute rounded petals. Our species of goldthread is common in mossy woods at all elevations in our

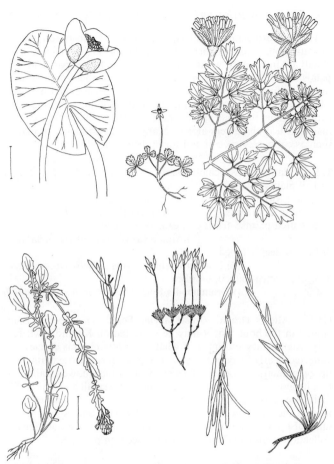

a. **Spatter-dock**
   Nuphar variegatum

b. **Goldthread**
   Coptis groenlandica

c. **Tall Meadow Rue**
   Thalictrum polygamum

d. **Northern Winter
   Cress**
   Barbarea orthoceras

e. **Allen's Draba**
   Draba Allenii

f. **Drummond's Rock
   Cress**
   Arabis Drummondi

area and it is often found above the trees. Its range is from Greenland to Manitoba and south to North Carolina and Iowa. A very similar species is found in Alaska and northern Asia. (Cankerroot.) Flowers are seen on Pl. 13, 3; an entire plant on p. 87, b.

CRUCIFERAE (Mustard Family)

The mustard family is a large one which is poorly represented on our mountains but much more common at lower elevations, chiefly by introduced weeds. The flower has four sepals and four petals; there are usually six stamens, two of them shorter than the other four; the fruit is a two-valved capsule called a *silique*. The structure of the siliques and the seed are important in identification but in the four species here treated identification can be made on leaf characters alone. Many of our common vegetables such as cabbage, broccoli and turnip belong to this family.

1. Low plants; leaves chiefly basal . . . . 2.
1. Tall plants; stems leafy . . . . 3.
    2. Mat-forming plants; fruits broadest at middle and tapering to both ends   (1) **Allen's Draba**   *Draba Allenii*
    2. Tufted plants; fruits elongate, cylindrical
                (3) **Alpine Cress**   *Cardamine bellidifolia*
3. Leaves deeply lobed
            (2) **Northern Winter Cress**   *Barbarea orthoceras*
3. Leaves lance-shaped, unlobed
            (4) **Drummond's Rock Cress**   *Arabis Drummondi*

(1)   **Allen's Draba**   *Draba Allenii* Fern. This species is included in the hope that it may be relocated on Katahdin where a very fragmentary specimen of what was probably this species was collected nearly forty years ago. The plant forms close mats made up of numerous rosettes of leaves from which flower stalks rise to a height of about 3 inches. The flowers are small and white. The fruits are smooth, flattened, broadest at the middle and tapering to each end. The species is known only from the Shickshock Mountains of the Gaspé Peninsula in Quebec plus this one questionable collection from Katahdin. A plant is seen on p. 87, e.

(2)   **Northern Winter Cress**   *Barbarea orthoceras* Ledeb. A somewhat similar situation to that of the previous species is found here. The only collection of this species in our area was made in Tuckerman Ravine on Mt. Washington in 1895. Several sheets exist of this collection, all being flowering material with no mature fruits. On the basis of leaf characters there seems little doubt that the identification is correct but it would be reassuring to find some mature fruiting plants. This species is very similar to the yellow rocket, a common weed at lower elevations in our area. It differs from the yellow rocket, *B. vulgaris*, in having the beak of the fruit

much shorter and in having the upper leaves of the stem bearing several pairs of narrow lobes cut in almost to the midrib. This species is found in Asia and from Labrador to Alaska south to the Fort Kent area in Maine and to Arizona and California along the mountains of the West. The fruits shown in the illustration are from material I collected in northern California. A flowering plant and fruit are seen on p. 87, d.

(3)   **Alpine Cress** *Cardamine bellidifolia* L. The alpine cress is a tiny plant with tufts of ovate leaves, white flowers, and slender, erect pods. It is found locally at the heads of ravines on Mt. Washington, Lafayette and Katahdin. The species is general through the arctic and alpine regions of the Northern Hemisphere. Leaves, a flower and fruits are seen on Pl. 14, 3.

(4)   **Drummond's Rock Cress** *Arabis Drummondi* Gray. This is a tall plant with entire lance-shaped leaves, white flowers, and ascending flattened, elongate pods. The entire plant is smooth. The species is found on ledges and talus slopes from Labrador to British Columbia south to Delaware in the East and down the mountains to New Mexico and California in the West. While not a real alpine it does occur in alpine ravines on all our major mountains. A fruiting plant is seen on p. 87, f.

DROSERACEAE (Sundew Family)

The sundew family is a small group of plants which usually grow in bogs and have highly specialized leaves which capture insects. The sundews can easily be recognized by the stalked glands present on the surface of the leaf. The Venus flytrap of the coastal plain of the Carolinas also belongs to this family and the pitcher-plant of our lowland bogs belongs to a closely related family.

Sundew *Drosera rotundifolia* L. The sundew is a common plant of bogs. The upper surfaces of the round leaves are covered with glandular hairs bearing drops at their tips which glisten like dew and function like flypaper in capturing insects. The flower stalks are leafless, and the inflorescence is nodding. The buds open in order from the base to the tip, and the open flower is always the highest point on the stem. The sundew is found throughout the Northern Hemisphere at moderate elevations and the plant is occasional well up in alpine ravines. In Scandinavia the leaves are used like rennet to thicken milk. Foliage is seen on Pl. 13, 2.

SAXIFRAGACEAE (Saxifrage Family)

The saxifrage family contains both herbs and shrubs. The leaves of all the species here treated are simple, although in some cases deeply cleft. The flowers of *Chrysosplenium* are built on a plan of four, those of *Saxifraga* and *Ribes* on a plan of five. The members of this family, with a few exceptions, do not form a conspicuous part of our vegetation even in the lowlands; a few such as the mock-orange and hydrangea are common cultivated shrubs. The saxifrages here described are all rather rare. *Chrysosplenium* and *Ribes* are much more common below treeline than above it.

1. Small herbs . . . . 2.
1. Shrubs of moderate size . . . . 5.
  2. Erect plants; leaves basal or alternate . . . . 3.
  2. Sprawling plants; leaves mostly opposite
          (4) **Golden Saxifrage** *Chrysosplenium americanum*
3. Leaves palmately lobed
          (2) **Alpine Brook Saxifrage** *Saxifraga rivularis*
3. Leaves not lobed . . . . 4.
  4. Leaves not encrusted with lime; flowers modified into tufts
    of small leaves   (1) **Star-like Saxifrage** *Saxifraga stellaris*
  4. Leaves toothed, a pore encrusted with lime at base of each
    tooth; flowers normal
          (3) **White Mountain-Saxifrage** *Saxifraga Aizoön*
5. Stem bearing prickles; fruit black
          (5) **Swamp Black Currant** *Ribes lacustre*
5. Stems without prickles; fruit red . . . . 6.
  6. Fruit bristly   (6) **Skunk Currant** *Ribes glandulosum*
  6. Fruit smooth   (7) **Red Currant** *Ribes triste*

(1)   **Star-like Saxifrage** *Saxifraga stellaris* L., var. *comosa* Poir. The star-like saxifrage is known from our area only on Katahdin. The thin green leaves are all basal. Most of the flowers are modified into tufts of small leaves which take root when detached from the parent plant but in large specimens the terminal flower may be normal and white. The species grows in mossy and springy places and is circumpolar in the high arctic; the Katahdin station is the only one in the United States. (Arctic saxifrage.) A plant is seen on Pl. 14, 2 and on p. 91, a.

(2)   **Alpine Brook Saxifrage** *Saxifraga rivularis* L. The alpine brook saxifrage is a small tufted plant with small white or pinkish flowers growing in moist areas in the upper reaches of ravines. It is a circumpolar arctic-alpine species which gets as far north as

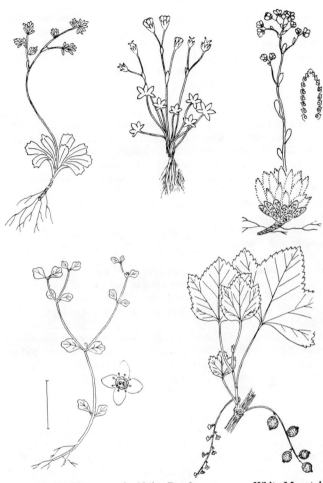

a. **Star-like Saxifrage**
Saxifraga stellaris,
var. *comosa*

b. **Alpine Brook Saxifrage**
Saxifraga rivularis

c. **White Mountain-Saxifrage**
Saxifraga Aizoön, var.
neogaea
plant and detail
of leaf

d. **Golden Saxifrage**
Chrysosplenium americanum

e. **Red Currant**
Ribes triste

91

latitude 83° in Greenland; in our area it is known only from Mt. Washington, where it is rather rare; it is also found in the mountains of Montana. In the Arctic it is a nitrophile, growing at the foot of bird cliffs and around human habitations, which may explain one of its colonies on Mt. Washington. A plant is seen on Pl. 13, 4 and on p. 91, b.

(3)   **White Mountain-Saxifrage** *Saxifraga Aizoön* Jacq., var. *neogaea* Butters. Notice the hyphen between mountain and saxifrage; the common name is given to differentiate this species from *S. aizoides*, the yellow mountain-saxifrage. The white mountain-saxifrage does not occur in the White Mountains being known from our area only on Katahdin and lowland cliffs in northern Vermont and New York. The lime-encrusted pores on the leaves make it an easy species to identify. The variety is found in the eastern Arctic of North America and south to our area, northern Michigan and northeast Minnesota. It is a plant of calcareous ledges and gravels. A plant and a detail of a leaf are seen on p. 91, c.

(4)   **Golden Saxifrage** *Chrysosplenium americanum* Schwein. The golden saxifrage carpets the mud of springheads and rills and while quite common at lower elevations is easily overlooked. The leaves are mostly opposite and the inconspicuous flowers lack petals. The species is found from Quebec to Saskatchewan and south to Georgia and Iowa. It is not an alpine species but since it grows in cold springs it does get well up on our mountains and has been collected in the Alpine Garden on Mt. Washington. A plant and an enlarged flower are seen on p. 91, d.

(5)   **Swamp Black Currant** *Ribes lacustre* (Pers.) Poir. In this species the stems are covered with prickles and the fruits are bristly and black. The crushed leaves of this and the next species have a somewhat skunk-like odor. It is found in cool woods and swamps from Newfoundland to Alaska and south to Tennessee and California. While more abundant at lower elevations it is frequent in our alpine areas. Foliage and fruit are seen on Pl. 15, 2.

(6)   **Skunk Currant** *Ribes glandulosum* Grauer. The skunk currant is named for the skunk-like odor of the bruised leaves and fruit. The branches lack prickles, the fruits are bristly and red. It is a low shrub of moist woods from Labrador to British Columbia and south to North Carolina and Minnesota. Like the previous species it is fairly frequent in our alpine areas. Foliage and fruit are seen on Pl. 15, 1.

(7)   **Red Currant** *Ribes triste* Pall. The branches of the red currant do not bear prickles and the red fruits are not bristly; the plant also lacks the skunky odor. The inflorescence spreads and droops more than does that of the skunk currant and the flowers tend to be purplish rather than whitish. This is another species of cool woods from Labrador to Alaska and south to West Virginia and Oregon; it is also found in Asia. Of the three currants it is the least abundant in our alpine areas. Foliage, flowers, and fruit are seen on p. 91, e.

ROSACEAE (Rose Family)

The members of this family are numerous, including herbs, shrubs and trees with a wide diversity of form. The leaves are alternate and may be simple or either pinnately or palmately compound. The flowers are regular and usually have numerous stamens. Most of the cultivated fruits of temperate regions belong to this family as do many of our cultivated shrubs. The native species and introduced weeds make up a prominent part of our lowland vegetation and the family is better represented than most above treeline.

1. Leaves simple . . . .   2.
1. Leaves composed of three or more leaflets . . . . . .   6.
  2. Leaves unlobed, longer than broad . . . .   3.
  2. Leaves distinctly lobed, as broad as long
        (14) **Baked-apple Berry** *Rubus Chamaemorus*
3. Flowers and fruits small and numerous, borne in a compact cluster, fruits not fleshy
        (1) **Northern Meadowsweet** *Spiraea latifolia*
3. Flowers and fruits larger, borne singly or a few in a loose cluster, fruits fleshy . . . .   4.
  4. Leaves usually broadest below the middle and tapering to a slender tip; the red fruit containing a single stone
        (17) **Wild Red Cherry** *Prunus pensylvanica*
  4. Leaves usually broadest near or above the middle, tip not slender; the purple-to-black fruits several to many seeded   5.
5. Leaves broadest above the middle and tapering to the base, glandular along the midrib and on the tips of the teeth; flowers and fruits in groups of five or more
        (2) **Black Chokeberry** *Pyrus melanocarpa*
5. Leaves usually broadest near the middle and tapering to each end, not glandular; flowers and fruits solitary or in groups of two or three (5) **Juneberry** *Amelanchier Bartramiana*
  6. Leaves pinnately compound (leaflets arranged like parts of a feather) . . . .   7.

93

6. Leaves palmately compound (leaflets arranged like fingers of a hand) . . . . 11.
7. Shrubs . . . . 8.
7. Herbs . . . . 10.
   8. Leaflets five to seven; flowers solitary or few, yellow
                   (8) **Shrubby Cinquefoil** *Potentilla fruticosa*
   8. Leaflets eleven to seventeen; flowers many, white . . . 9.
9. Leaflets lance-shaped, tapering to a sharp tip
               (3) **American Mountain Ash** *Pyrus americana*
9. Leaflets broader, rounded gradually to a point
                (4) **Shrubby Mountain Ash** *Pyrus decora*
  10. Terminal leaflet of basal leaves three-lobed, some lateral
     leaflets long, others short; flowers nodding, purplish
                  (12) **Purple Avens** *Geum rivale*
  10 Terminal leaflet of basal leaves rounded, kidney-shaped,
     lateral leaflets all short; flowers ascending, yellow
               (13) **Mountain Avens** *Geum Peckii*
11. Fruits fleshy; flowers white . . . . 12.
11. Fruits dry; flowers yellow in all but one species . . . . 14.
  12. Stemless plants; fruit a strawberry
               (6) **Wild Strawberry** *Fragaria virginiana*
  12. Stemmed plants; fruit a raspberry . . . . 13.
13. Low unarmed plants (15) **Dwarf Raspberry** *Rubus pubescens*
13. Taller plants with prickles (16) **Wild Raspberry** *Rubus idaeus*
  14. Smooth plants with white flowers
         (9) **Three-toothed Cinquefoil** *Potentilla tridentata*
  14. Hairy plants with yellow flowers . . . . 15.
15. Low plants; leaflets three- to five-toothed at tip . . . . 16.
15. Erect plants with leafy stems; leaflets with more than five
    teeth   (10) **Rough Cinquefoil** *Potentilla norvegica*
  16. Minute plants less than one inch tall; stamens numerous
         (11) **Dwarf Cinquefoil** *Potentilla Robbinsiana*
  16. Plants more than one inch tall; stamens five
          (7) **Sibbaldia** *Sibbaldia procumbens*

(1)   **Northern Meadowsweet** *Spiraea latifolia* (Ait.) Borkh.,
var. *septentrionalis* Fern. Most readers are probably familiar with
meadowsweet and the closely related steeple-bush in the pastures
throughout our area. A variety of the meadowsweet occurs above
treeline at the heads of ravines and in alpine meadows. In the
lowland variety the lower branches of the inflorescence are relatively long giving the inflorescence a pyramidal shape. In the alpine
variety the branches are short so that the inflorescence is oval or
cylindrical. The alpine variety is found from Labrador to Ungava

and south to the alpine regions of Katahdin and the White Mountains, the mountains of northern Virginia and the Keweenaw Peninsula in Michigan. The lowland var. *latifolia* may also occasionally be found fairly high on the mountains. The foliage and inflorescence are seen on Pl. 15, 3.

(2)   **Black Chokeberry** *Pyrus melanocarpa* (Michx.) Willd. The chokeberry is a shrub of moderate height with white flowers and black berry-like fruit. There are three species in the group and they are sometimes difficult to separate. Collections indicate that *P. melanocarpa* is the one most likely to be found at high elevations. In this species the branchlets and under surfaces of the leaves are smooth. The black chokeberry is found from Newfoundland to Minnesota and south to Tennessee. The purple chokeberry, *P. floribunda*, with pubescent branchlets and leaves may possibly also be found on the mountains. Twigs with flowers and fruit are seen on p. 97, a.

(3)   **American Mountain Ash** *Pyrus americana* (Marsh.) DC. Both species of mountain ash are much more common in the lower woods but a few individuals are found beyond the limits of most trees. They are shrubs or small trees with pinnately compound leaves, white flowers and orange-red fruit. The leaflets in this species are narrow and lance-shaped and taper to a point. The American mountain ash is found over about the same range as the black chokeberry. (Roundwood, dogberry, missey-moosey.) The autumn foliage is seen on Pl. 15, 4.

(4)   **Shrubby Mountain Ash** *Pyrus decora* (Sarg.) Hyland. The shrubby mountain ash differs from the previous species in having shorter and broader leaflets which are rounded to the summit. Where both species grow together this species flowers about ten days later than the other. Its range extends from Greenland to Manitoba and south to New England, New York and Minnesota. It is probably the commoner species at high elevations. No one except a botanist would suspect that the mountain ash belongs to the same genus as the pear, apple, and chokeberry. Some botanists split the genus into four smaller ones, the chokeberry being placed in *Aronia* and the mountain ash in *Sorbus*. Foliage and fruit are seen on p. 99, a.

(5)   **Juneberry** *Amelanchier Bartramiana* (Tausch) Roemer. Juneberries or shadbushes as a whole are bad when it comes to identification. *A. Bartramiana*, however, is easily recognized since it bears its white flowers singly or a few in a cluster instead of having many-flowered clusters. The leaves are thin, flat, sharp-pointed

and of a dull green color. The fruits are deep purple and covered by a bloom. The species is found from Labrador to New England and westward to the Great Lakes. It is common in the peaty and damp thickets of our area and it frequently grows at the higher elevations. (Sugarplum, shadbush, serviceberry.) A flowering branch is seen on Pl. 16, 1.

(6)   **Wild Strawberry**   *Fragaria virginiana* Duchesne, var. *terra-novae* (Rydb.) Fern. & Wieg. The wild strawberry, common in the lowlands, is undoubtedly known to most readers. Occasional plants will be found on the upper slopes of the alpine ravines but not in sufficient quantities to provide a good meal. A flowering plant is seen on Pl. 16, 2.

(7)   **Sibbaldia**   *Sibbaldia procumbens* L. Sibbaldia is closely related to the cinquefoils from which it differs in having only five stamens and ten or fewer achenes. It is a low, slightly hairy plant with three-parted leaves, each leaflet having three teeth at the apex. It is a circumpolar subarctic and alpine plant which extends well south along the mountains of the West. In our area it occurs only on Mt. Washington where it is rare; in fact I know of only one small colony and that is fortunately far from any trail. A flowering plant is seen on Pl. 16, 3.

(8)   **Shrubby Cinquefoil**   *Potentilla fruticosa* L. This is our only woody member of the genus and also the only one which has five leaflets, the leaves being pinnately compound instead of palmately as in the other species treated here. The species has a circumboreal distribution and is widespread in North America, being found from Labrador to Alaska and south to Tennessee and Arizona. At low elevations in our area it is an occasional species growing in open places and on cliffs. It has been found in Huntington Ravine on Mt. Washington and may well occur in similar habitats on other mountains of the region. Flowers and foliage are seen on p. 97, b.

(9)   **Three-toothed Cinquefoil**   *Potentilla tridentata* Ait. The three-toothed cinquefoil is our only species with white flowers. The main stem is creeping and subterranean; the flowering branches are erect with three-parted mostly basal leaves. The leaflets are smooth and have three teeth at the apex. It is the most common cinquefoil in the alpine regions of our area. Its total range extends from Greenland to the Mackenzie and south to Georgia and North Dakota. While it is usually found in rocky and gravelly areas on the mountains it also occurs on ledges along the seacoast as far as Marblehead, Massachusetts. An enlarged flower is seen on Pl. 17, 1 and the plant on 17, 3.

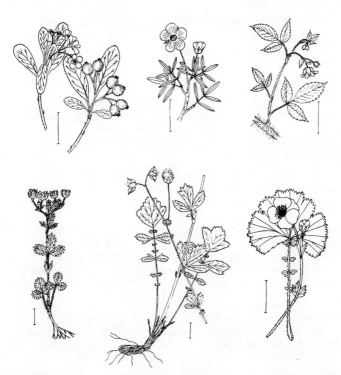

a. **Black Chokeberry**
   Pyrus melanocarpa

b. **Shrubby Cinquefoil**
   Potentilla fruticosa

c. **Wild Raspberry**
   Rubus idaeus

d. **Rough Cinquefoil**
   Potentilla norvegica

e. **Purple Avens**
   Geum rivale

f. **Mountain Avens**
   Geum Peckii

(10) **Rough Cinquefoil** *Potentilla norvegica* L. The rough cinquefoil is an erect hairy species with three-parted leaves and yellow flowers. The leaflets are coarsely several-toothed. The species is circumboreal and is widespread in North America, where it is probably both a native species and an introduced weed. It is a variable species which grows in quite diverse habitats. The northern and alpine plants have been segregated as var. *labradorica* (Lehm.) Fern., which is characterized as having the stems glabrous and the leaves nearly so. The rough cinquefoil is occasional in our alpine areas and many of the collections I have studied are quite pubescent. The plant is seen on p. 97, d.

(11) **Dwarf Cinquefoil** *Potentilla Robbinsiana* Oakes. The dwarf cinquefoil is probably the rarest plant to be found on the Presidential Range. It is a very small and inconspicuous plant whose yellow flowers are gone by the first of July. In the past it has been confused with *P. frigida* of the higher mountains of Europe to which it is closely related. The species is known only from the White Mountains and there it is limited to an area of a few acres on Mt. Washington and to the Franconia Range. According to Frederic Steele one of the two stations in the Franconias is now apparently extinct and the other is reduced to two plants. The plant is seen on Pl. 14, 5.

(12) **Purple Avens** *Geum rivale* L. The purple avens is a frequent plant of wet meadows and bogs of our area at low elevations and it is occasionally found at the heads of alpine ravines. The flowers are nodding and both the sepals and the petals tend to be purple. The styles of the fruit are quite conspicuous. The species occurs from Labrador to British Columbia and south to West Virginia and New Mexico. It is also found in the boreal portions of Eurasia. (Water avens, chocolate-root.) The flower is seen on Pl. 17, 2; the entire plant on p. 97, e.

(13) **Mountain Avens** *Geum Peckii* Pursh. The mountain avens has large buttercup-like flowers which are among the showiest blossoms to be found above timberline. The foliage resembles slightly the leaves of galax which garnish bunches of hothouse violets. The mountain avens is restricted to the White Mountain area and one island in western Nova Scotia. It is common in the alpine areas and has a few lowland stations. It is closely related to *G. radiatum* of the mountains of North Carolina and Tennessee and to *G. calthifolium* of the North Pacific region. The flower is seen on Pl. 17, 4; the foliage and flower on p. 97, f.

(14) **Baked-apple Berry** *Rubus Chamaemorus* L. The genus *Rubus* has fortunately only three species which are likely to be encountered above treeline and we are spared the intricacies of the blackberry complex. It is more characteristic of barren tops of lower mountains than of alpine areas but it does occur at the heads of some ravines. The plants are less than a foot tall, with fairly large white flowers and amber-colored fruits resembling raspberries. The species is found in bogs throughout the Arctic. In the West it does not extend into the United States. In the East it extends southward along the coast to eastern Maine and an isolated station on Montauk Point, Long Island; it also reaches the mountains of western Maine and the White Mountains. In Newfoundland the

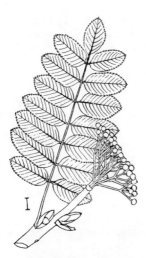 

a. **Shrubby Mountain Ash**
Pyrus decora

b. **Wild Red Cherry**
Prunus pensylvanica

fruits are gathered regularly and used as food. (Cloudberry.) The flower and foliage are seen on Pl. 17, 5.

(15)   **Dwarf Raspberry**   *Rubus pubescens* Raf. The dwarf raspberry is found well up in the alpine ravines and meadows. The plants are somewhat taller than those of the previous species; the leaves are compound; and the flowers are smaller and often have one or two extra petals. The fruits are raspberry-like, but not readily detached from the bush. The species extends from Labrador to British Columbia and southward into the United States in cool, damp woods. The foliage and fruit are shown on Pl. 16, 4.

(16)   **Wild Raspberry**   *Rubus idaeus* L. The common wild raspberry is probably familiar to most readers. It is abundant at lower elevations in our area and extends well up on the mountains. The species has been split into a number of varieties which are difficult to separate. The two most likely to be found on the mountains are var. *strigosus* (Michx.) Maxim. which has the bark of the first-year canes smooth beneath the bristles and var. *canadensis* Richards. which has the bark of the first-year canes pubescent beneath the bristles. The species is native to Europe; one or more varieties are found over much of temperate North America. A flowering twig is shown on p. 97, c.

(17) **Wild Red Cherry** *Prunus pensylvanica* L. f. The wild red cherry is often called the fire cherry because it is one of the first trees to grow in burned-over areas. Very common lower down, some individuals are found on the floors and headwalls of the ravines. The flowers are typical wild cherry flowers and the fruits are small and red. The species extends from Labrador to British Columbia and southward along the mountains to Colorado in the West, and to North Carolina and Tennessee in the East. A fruiting branch is shown on p. 99, b.

OXALIDACEAE (Wood-sorrel Family)

Most of the members of this family are in the genus *Oxalis*. All the members of this genus in our area have characteristic three-parted, palmately compound leaves. The flowers are regular and on a plan of five, the fruit is a capsule. The sour juice of the plants is characteristic. While the wood sorrel has white flowers most of our species have smaller yellow blossoms.

Common Wood Sorrel *Oxalis montana* Raf. The wood sorrels have three-parted, somewhat clover-like compound leaves. Each naked flower stalk bears a single blossom with white petals which have purple veins. The leaves when chewed are acid and refreshing. The wood sorrel is found in cool woods from Newfoundland to Manitoba and south to the mountains of North Carolina and Tennessee. Like the goldthread, this species is sometimes found under clumps of alpine scrub. (Wood shamrock.) A plant is shown on Pl. 17, 6.

CALLITRICHACEAE (Water-starwort Family)

This family contains only the genus *Callitriche*. Most of the species are inconspicuous aquatic plants growing in shallow water. The submersed leaves are usually slender and elongate; many of the species also produce rosettes of broader and shorter floating leaves which may almost cover woodland pools. The flowers are borne in the leaf axils and are very small and simple. The male flower consists of a single stamen and the female of a single pistil. Mature fruits are needed for proper identification of species. The Callitriches are generally ignored except by a few specialists in the genus.

Water-Starwort *Callitriche anceps* Fern. The water-starworts are a genus of small, slender aquatic plants with narrow elongate submersed leaves and shorter and broader floating leaves. The flowers are very small and the identification of species is based largely on the structure of the mature fruits which are also small and must be studied with a fairly powerful hand-lens. Most amateurs never even notice the entire plant. *C. anceps* is the only species likely to be encountered in high alpine pools. The species is found from Greenland to New England and New York plus a few widely scattered stations. A fruiting stem is shown on p. 102, a.

EMPETRACEAE (Crowberry Family)

This family consists of three genera of shrubs which have flowers lacking petals and in some lacking sepals. All the genera are small in number of species. The relationship of the family is still in doubt, some consider it to be a degenerate relative of the heaths. *Empetrum* is found throughout the colder parts of the Northern Hemisphere; the other two genera, *Corema* and *Ceratiola*, are restricted to the eastern portion of North America.

1. Berries black; young branches and margins of leaves glandular
  (1) **Black Crowberry** *Empetrum nigrum*
1. Berries red to purplish-black; young branches and leaf margins hairy but not glandular
  (2) **Purple Crowberry** *Empetrum atropurpureum*

(1)   **Black Crowberry** *Empetrum nigrum* L. The crowberry is a low plant whose appearance resembles slightly a hair-cap moss. The flowers are very small, lacking petals, and are seldom noticed although the stamens may be seen if the plants are examined closely. The black crowberry has small black fruit, hence the common name. It is a widespread species in the arctic regions of both the Old World and the New and it extends southward on the mountains and along the coast. It has been collected in northern Greenland within ten degrees of the North Pole. It is common on the mountains of Maine, New Hampshire and New York but less common on the Vermont mountains. (Curlewberry.) Male flowers are shown on Pl. 20, 1; fruit on 20, 2.

(2)   **Purple Crowberry** *Empetrum atropurpureum* Fern. & Wieg. The two species of crowberry can easily be separated by the color of the berry even though the plants look very similar. The purple crowberry is not an arctic plant, growing from Labrador to Lake Mistassini, Quebec, and south to the mountains of Maine and New Hampshire. On our mountains it is less abundant than the black crowberry and does not usually occur at such high elevations as the previous species. An enlarged leaf of *E. nigrum* (N.) and of *E. atropurpureum* (A.) is shown on p. 102, b.

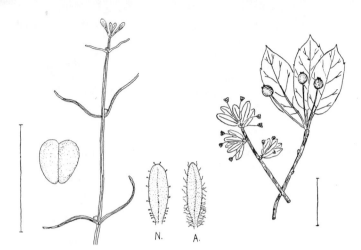

a. **Water-Starwort**
Callitriche anceps

b. **Crowberry**
Empetrum
N. leaf *E. nigrum*
A. leaf *E. atropurpureum*

c. **Mountain Holly**
Nemopanthus
mucronatus

AQUIFOLIACEAE (Holly Family)

This is another family containing only three genera, but the number of species is greater than in the previous family. *Nemopanthus* contains only the mountain holly; *Ilex* is a much larger genus and includes the American holly and the black alder. All members of the family are trees or shrubs; the leaves are usually alternate; the fruits are berry-like drupes.

Mountain Holly *Nemopanthus mucronata* (L.) Trel. The mountain holly is a common shrub of damp woods which occurs well up on our mountains. The leaves are thin and have few if any teeth. The flowers are inconspicuous and open as the leaves expand. The fruits are berry-like and red. The species occurs from Newfoundland to Minnesota and south to West Virginia and Indiana. (Catberry.) Foliage, flowers, and fruit are shown on p. 102, c.

ACERACEAE (Maple Family)

This is a family of trees and shrubs confined to the Northern Hemisphere. It contains two genera but most of the species are

a. **Mountain Maple**
Acer spicatum

b. **Striped Maple**
Acer pensylvanicum

in the genus *Acer*, which includes the maples. The maple leaves are opposite and in most species palmately lobed and veined but in the box-elder of our lowlands they are pinnately compound. The fruits are winged keys or samaras.

1. Flowers small and petals inconspicuous; leaf margins coarsely toothed   (1) **Mountain Maple**   *Acer spicatum*
1. Flowers larger and yellow petals more conspicuous; leaf margins finely toothed   (2) **Striped Maple**   *Acer pensylvanicum*

(1)   **Mountain Maple**   *Acer spicatum* Lam. Both maples are common shrubs or small trees along the trails up our mountains. The mountain maple is the smaller of the two, the bark is drab, the leaves are coarsely toothed and the flowers are small and relatively inconspicuous. Mountain maple is found in cool woods from Newfoundland to Saskatchewan and south to Georgia and Iowa. It probably does not occur much above 3500 feet on our mountains. Foliage, flowers and fruit are shown on p. 103, a.

(2)   **Striped Maple**   *Acer pensylvanicum* L. The striped maple or moosewood is a showier shrub. The bark is frequently green with white stripes, the leaves are larger and more finely toothed and the flowers are much larger and have yellow petals. It occurs from Nova Scotia to Manitoba and south to Georgia and Michigan. Its altitudinal range in our mountains is about the same as that

103

of the mountain maple. (Goosefoot-maple, whistlewood, he-moosewood.) Foliage, flowers and fruit are shown on p. 103, b.

VIOLACEAE (Violet Family)

The violet family is world-wide in its distribution and while our native violets are relatively small herbs some of the tropical members of the family are trees and shrubs. Some of our violets are stemless plants, the leaves and flowers arising directly from the rhizome; others have definite stems bearing the leaves and flowers. Many violets produce two types of blossoms. The conspicuous spring flowers are familiar to most readers. Flowers of the other type are often hidden under the leaves or even underground; they are apetalous and never open. These flowers are said to be cleistogamous and they are self-fertilized. The identification of violets is difficult, since closely allied species hybridize freely and all sorts of intermediate plants are frequently collected.

1. Leaves all basal . . . . 2.
1. Stems leafy; flowers violet
                      (5) **American Dog Violet**   *Viola adunca*
  2. Flowers violet or lilac . . . . 3.
  2. Flowers blue or white . . . . 4.
  3. Spur of flower long; leaves short-hairy; rootstock not
    creeping   (2) **Great-spurred Violet**   *Viola Selkirkii*
  3. Spur of flower short; leaves smooth; rootstock creeping
             (3) **Northern Marsh Violet**   *Viola palustris*
    4. Flowers blue, on very long stalks; rootstocks not creeping
           (1) **Blue Marsh Violet**   *Viola cucullata*
    4. Flowers white, on stalks of moderate length; rootstocks
    creeping   (4) **Wild White Violet**   *Viola pallens*

(1)   **Blue Marsh Violet**   *Viola cucullata* Ait. This is the largest and most conspicuous of the violets treated here. The leaves are often over 6 inches tall and the flowers overtop the leaves. The blue marsh violet is common in swamps and bogs at lower elevations in our area and occasionally is found as high as 4000 feet on the mountains. It is a widespread species found from Newfoundland to Ontario and south to Georgia and Arkansas. A plant is shown on p. 105, b.

(2)   **Great-spurred Violet**   *Viola Selkirkii* Pursh. The greatspurred violet may be distinguished by the long spur on the violet-colored flower; by the hairy upper surfaces of the leaves, by having the basal lobes of the leaves in contact with each other or

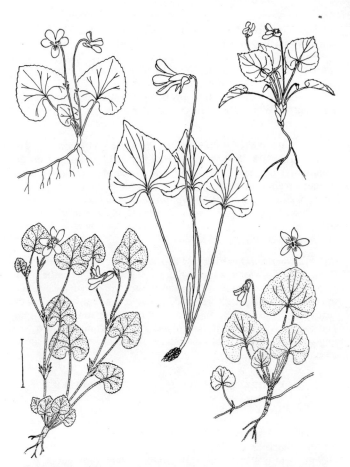

a. **Wild White Violet**   b. **Blue Marsh Violet**   c. **Great-spurred Violet**
   Viola pallens   *Viola cucullata*   *Viola Selkirkii*

d. **American Dog Violet**   e. **Northern Marsh Violet**
   Viola adunca, var. *minor*   *Viola palustris*

overlapping; and by the absence of creeping rootstocks or stolons.
It is a violet of rich, usually deciduous, woods at lower elevations
and is not common on our mountains but it has been found at
4000 feet on Katahdin. It is a circumboreal species which extends
south in North America to Pennsylvania and Colorado. A plant
is shown on p. 105, c.

(3)   **Northern Marsh Violet**   *Viola palustris* L. The northern marsh violet has violet flowers with a short spur; the leaves are not hairy and the basal lobes do not meet; it has slender creeping rootstocks. It has a circumpolar distribution in the subarctic and extends south to the mountains of Maine and New Hampshire, Colorado and Oregon. It is probably the most common alpine violet in the White Mountains. A flower is shown on Pl. 19, 1; a plant on p. 105, e.

(4)   **Wild White Violet**   *Viola pallens* (Banks) Brainerd. This is the only white flowered violet that one is likely to find on our mountains; the leaves are smooth and the basal lobes do not meet; slender creeping rootstocks are present. It is the common white violet of our area at lower elevations and it is occasionally found at or close to treeline. *V. pallens* occurs from Labrador to Alaska and south to Alabama and North Dakota. A flower is shown on Pl. 19, 2; a plant on p. 105, a.

(5)   **American Dog Violet**   *Viola adunca* Sm., var. *minor* (Hook.) Fern. The dog violet is the only leafy-stemmed violet to be found high on our mountains. The flowers are violet; the leaves are smooth; and the plants are tufted. It is occasionally found at the heads of alpine ravines and is less common at lower elevations. The species is found from Greenland to Alaska and south to New England, New York, Colorado and California. A plant is shown on p. 105, d.

ONAGRACEAE (Evening-primrose Family)

This is a fairly large family in which the basic plan of the flower is usually four. It includes the evening-primroses and a number of less conspicuous genera with us, and a number of showy genera in the West such as *Clarkia* and *Zauschneria*; the cultivated genus *Fuchsia* is also a member of this family. The only genus represented on the mountains of our area is *Epilobium* which has the typical four-parted flowers, a long slender capsule, and seeds which bear a tuft or coma of hairs at the summit. The fireweed is a large conspicuous species but most of the others treated here are rather small and not showy.

1. Tall plants, the stems terminating in a group of numerous
    large magenta flowers   (1) **Fireweed**   *Epilobium angustifolium*
1. Stems shorter and weak; flowers inconspicuous . . . . . 2.
    2. Leaf margins not toothed . . . . 3.
    2. Leaf margins toothed   . . . . 4.

3. Leaves tapering to the tip
(2) **Marsh Willow-herb** *Epilobium palustre*
3. Leaves broadly rounded at tip
(5) **Pimpernel-leaved Willow-herb** *Epilobium anagallidifolium*
4. Upper leaves usually longer than the internodes; flowers usually pink or violet
(3) **Hornemann's Willow-herb** *Epilobium Hornemanni*
4. Upper leaves usually shorter than the internodes; flowers usually white   (4) **Alpine Willow-herb** *Epilobium alpinum*

(1)   **Fireweed** *Epilobium angustifolium* L. The fireweed is one of the most common plants in the Northern Hemisphere. Its small tufted seeds are blown long distances by the wind, and the species soon occupies burned-over areas and transforms them in the summer into masses of magenta blooms. The new shoots may be used as a substitute for asparagus, and the Indians of the Northwest use the pith of the larger stems as a thickening in soup. Any amount used as food will make no impression on the numbers of the plants. While in no sense an alpine the species is occasionally found above timberline. (Great willow-herb, wickup, blooming-Sally.) The flowers are shown on Pl. 18, 1.

(2)   **Marsh Willow-herb** *Epilobium palustre* L. The willow-herbs are a difficult group of species to identify with certainty. The marsh willow-herb has leaves with untoothed margins which are often inrolled. The stems are rather weak. The flowers are pink or white, and the stalks of the fruit are much shorter than the pods. The species is found over much of the cooler portion of the Northern Hemisphere. A number of intergrading varieties have been described and several of them occur in the alpine areas of our region. The plant is shown on Pl. 18, 3 and on p. 108, a.

(3)   **Hornemann's Willow-herb** *Epilobium Hornemanni* Reichenb. Hornemann's willow-herb has leaves with widely spaced minute teeth on the margins. The upper leaves are usually longer than the internodes. The flowers are pink or violet; and the seeds, when viewed with a microscope, are papillose. The species is circumboreal, in damp soil. It occurs on Katahdin, the White Mountains and the Adirondacks in the East and on the higher mountains of the West. Flowers are shown on Pl. 18, 2; the entire plant on p. 108, b.

(4)   **Alpine Willow-herb** *Epilobium alpinum* L. The alpine willow-herb also has leaves with toothed margins but the upper leaves are usually shorter than the internodes, the flowers are white,

a. **Marsh Willow-herb**
   Epilobium palustre

b. **Hornemann's Willow-herb**
   Epilobium Hornemanni

c. **Alpine Willow-herb**
   Epilobium alpinum

d. **Pimpernel-leaved Willow-herb**
   Epilobium anagallidifolium

and the seeds, under magnification, are smooth. The habitat and range of this species are about the same as that of Hornemann's willow-herb. In the East it occurs on Katahdin and the White Mountains. The plant is shown on p. 108, c.

(5)   **Pimpernel-leaved Willow-herb**   *Epilobium anagallidifolium* Lam. This is the smallest of our willow-herbs. The slender stems are usually curved and arching, the leaves are untoothed and broadly rounded at the tip, the flowers are pink or purple, and the seeds are smooth. The general range is similar to that of the previous two species but in our area it is known only from Katahdin. The plant is shown on p. 108, d.

ARALIACEAE (Ginseng Family)

Most of the members of this family are tropical; of about sixty genera only four occur naturally in the United States. The various members differ greatly in appearance ranging from the Hercules'-

club and devil's-club which are large and very spiny shrubs or trees, to English ivy which is a vine, to the dwarf ginseng which is a tiny herb. In all, the flowers are numerous and borne in an umbel, the basic plan of the flower is five, and the fruit is a berry-like drupe.

Wild Sarsaparilla   *Aralia nudicaulis* L. The wild sarsaparilla looks like no other plant in our area. The stem terminates just above ground level; a single large compound leaf rises from the stem as does a tall naked flower-stalk bearing at its summit two to seven globular heads of flowers or black berries, depending on the season. The species is common in the woods at lower elevations and is occasionally found up to about 4000 feet on the mountains. The range of the wild sarsaparilla extends from Labrador to British Columbia and south to Georgia and Colorado. The plant is shown on Pl. 18, 4.

UMBELLIFERAE (Parsley Family)

This is a large family of mostly herbaceous plants which frequently contain strong-smelling juices. Several are highly poisonous when eaten, for example the poison hemlock given to Socrates. The family contains some of our important vegetables, such as carrots, parsnips and celery; others such as anise, dill and caraway are used as flavorings; and some are used as drugs. The flowers are small and borne in umbels. The fruits vary widely in their appearance and are more useful than the flowers in making identifications. In the West many species are present and the family is a difficult one. The comparatively few species which occur in our area do not present such a problem.

1. Leaves divided into many leaflets; stems smooth
(1) Great Angelica   Angelica atropurpurea
1. Leaves divided into three broad leaflets; stems grooved
   and woolly   (2) **Cow Parsnip**   *Heracleum maximum*

(1)   **Great Angelica**   *Angelica atropurpurea* L. The great angelica can grow to a height of more than 6 feet. The leaves are large and divided into many leaflets. The compound umbel of flowers or fruits is roughly globular. The stems, after boiling in two waters, are said to resemble stewed celery. The young stems may be candied by cooking them in sugar syrup after boiling them in water. The plant is found in damp places from Labrador to Minnesota and south to West Virginia and Illinois. It is frequent in our area at lower elevations and also occurs at the heads of

a. **Great Angelica**
Angelica atropurpurea

b. **Cow Parsnip**
Heracleum maximum

alpine ravines. (Alexanders.) The foliage and fruit are shown on p. 110, a.

(2)   **Cow Parsnip**   *Heracleum maximum* Bartr. The cow parsnip attains about the same size as the angelica. The coarse stem is grooved and woolly, the leaves are divided into three large maple-like leaflets, the leaf sheaths are conspicuously inflated, the compound umbel is umbrella-like rather than globular. The boiled stalks and roots are eaten by some of the northern Indians. The water should be changed at least once to eliminate some of the strong flavor. The species is found from Labrador to Alaska and south in the mountains to Georgia and New Mexico. It is frequent at low levels in our area in meadows and is also found in alpine ravines. (Masterwort, cowcabbage.) The foliage and fruit are shown on p. 110, b.

CORNACEAE (Dogwood Family)

This is a small family of herbs, shrubs and trees which is chiefly tropical, only the genus *Cornus* being found in the United States. These dogwoods have no connection with the poison dogwood or poison sumac. The name "dogwood" is apparently derived from the fact that the wood of one of the European species is hard and is used for making meat skewers. The Old English word *dagge*

110

means dagger, this led to *dagwood* and finally to *dogwood*. In this family the flowers are small and borne in an umbel, the leaves are simple and usually opposite, the fruit is a berry-like drupe.

Bunchberry *Cornus canadensis* L. The bunchberry is probably familiar to most readers. The flowers are small and four-parted and the head of flowers is surrounded by four conspicuous white bracts which are sometimes mistaken for petals. The fruits are red berries. The berries, while not poisonous, are insipid and seldom eaten, but those of the more northern *C. suecica* are used in Lapland to make a dessert. Bunchberry occurs from Greenland to Alaska and south to West Virginia and New Mexico. A very common plant at lower elevations in our area it is also frequent about the margins of alpine scrub. (Dwarf cornel, crackerberry, pigeonberry, puddingberry.) The inflorescence is shown on Pl. 19, 4; the leaves and fruit on 19, 6.

PYROLACEAE (Wintergreen Family)

The wintergreen family differs from the heath family in that its members are herbaceous or nearly so while the heaths are shrubs; it is perhaps better to consider it a subfamily of the heaths. The wintergreen family can be subdivided into two groups. One group, represented with us by pipsissewa and the pyrolas, has well-developed green leaves. The members of the other group are saprophytes or root-parasites and lack chlorophyll, the stems tend to be fleshy and the leaves are reduced to scales. The Indian pipe belongs to the latter group.

Indian Pipe *Monotropa uniflora* L. The Indian pipe is also known as the corpse plant because of the waxy-white color of the entire plant when fresh. The plant is a saprophyte, getting its food from decaying organic matter in the soil rather than manufacturing it by photosynthesis. It is a wide-ranging species found in Asia and over much of North America south to Mexico. It is common in woodland humus of our area at lower elevations and may occasionally be found up to about 4000 feet on the mountains. (Convulsion-root, fits-root.) The plant is shown on Pl. 20, 3.

ERICACEAE (Heath Family)

The heath family includes many of the characteristic plants found above treeline. They are all shrubs; the leaves tend to be thick and somewhat leathery; the petals of the flower are united into a tube, at least at the base. The heaths are able to grow in acid sterile

111

soil not suited to many plants and some of them are found in bogs where the soil is always saturated with water. While the region above timberline all too often seems extremely moist to the climber, the plants found growing there may really be living under almost desert conditions. The nearly continuous winds blowing across the plants steadily remove water from the leaves. The roots have difficulty taking in water because of the acidity and the low temperature of the soil. Thus there is a constant struggle to take in water rapidly enough to replace that lost by the leaves. In many heaths the leaves possess structures which help to reduce water loss. Many of the species have evergreen leaves, which is an advantage to plants living where the growing season is short, since the leaves can manufacture food whenever conditions are favorable and no time is lost in expanding a set of leaves at the start of the growing season. Many of the heaths blossom early in the season and the flowers are not seen by summer climbers. The peak of the flowering season in our area is usually between the middle of June and the fourth of July.

1. Fruit berry-like . . . . . · . . . . 11.
1. Fruit not berry-like . . . . 2.
  2. Flowers white . . . . 3.
  2. Flowers colored . . . . 6.
3. Plants more than 6 inches tall . . . . 4.
3. Plants less than 6 inches tall, moss-like with needle-like leaves   (10) **Moss Plant** *Cassiope hypnoides*
  4. Flowers in umbel-like clusters; under side of leaves covered with white or rusty wool
          (1) **Labrador Tea** *Ledum groenlandicum*
  4. Flowers not in umbel-like clusters; leaves not woolly . . 5·
5. Leaves long and narrow, whitened beneath
        (8) **Bog Rosemary** *Andromeda glaucophylla*
5. Leaves one quarter to one half as broad as long; scurfy beneath   (9) **Leather-leaf** *Chamaedaphne calyculata*
  6. Plants usually at least 6 inches tall . . . . 7.
  6. Dwarf plants less than 6 inches tall . . . . 9.
7. Leaves alternate; flowers large, deeply cleft into three segments   (3) **Rhodora** *Rhododendron canadense*
7. Leaves opposite or ternate; flowers smaller, shallowly five-notched . . . . 8.
  8. Leaves broad and flat; inflorescence lateral
         (5) **Sheep Laurel** *Kalmia angustifolia*
  8. Leaves narrow with inrolled margins; inflorescence terminal   (6) **Pale Laurel** *Kalmia polifolia*

9. Mat-like plants; flowers erect, not cylindrical . . . . . 10.
9. Moss-like plants; flowers nodding, cylindrical
(7) **Mountain Heath** *Phyllodoce caerulea*
10. Plants scurfy; leaves relatively broad; flowers large, with
exserted stamens
(2) **Lapland Rosebay** *Rhododendron lapponicum*
10. Plants smooth; leaves narrow; flowers small with included stamens (4) **Alpine Azalea** *Loiseleuria procumbens*
11. Berries white, purple or red . . . . 12.
11. Berries blue to blue-black . . . . 15.
12. Berries white or purple . . . . 13.
12. Berries red . . . . 14.
13. Leaves broadest at the middle and tapering to either end;
berries white (11) **Creeping Snowberry** *Gaultheria hispidula*
13. Leaves broadest above the middle, apex broadly rounded;
berries purple (12) **Alpine Bearberry** *Arctostaphylos alpina*
14. Tufted plants; flowers and fruits borne in clusters on
short stems; flowers bell-shaped
(17) **Mountain Cranberry** *Vaccinium Vitis-Idaea*
14. Slender vine-like plants; flowers and fruits solitary on
long stalks; flowers with four reflexed petals
(18) **Wren's Egg Cranberry** *Vaccinium Oxycoccos*
15. Flowers and fruits solitary or in clusters of two or three . 16.
15. Flowers and fruits numerous in clusters . . . . 17.
16. Leaves entire; some of flowers and fruits in clusters of
two or three, fruits blue-black
(13) **Bog Bilberry** *Vaccinium uliginosum*
16. Leaves finely toothed; flowers and fruits solitary; fruits
light blue (14) **Dwarf Bilberry** *Vaccinium cespitosum*
17. Young branches and under or both surfaces of leaves hairy;
leaves entire
(15) **Velvet-leaf Blueberry** *Vaccinium myrtilloides*
17. Essentially smooth plants; leaves minutely toothed
(16) **Low Sweet Blueberry** *Vaccinium angustifolium*

(1) **Labrador Tea** *Ledum groenlandicum* Oeder. The Labrador tea is one of the taller heaths, and its thick leaves with the dense
brown woolly coating beneath are wholly unlike the leaves of any
other mountain plant. The erect white flowers with almost separate
petals may be seen in the early summer. The fruits are slender capsules. The plant is not restricted to the region above timberline,
being found also in cold bogs and wet thickets in the lowlands.
As the scientific name implies, the Labrador tea is native to Greenland as well as to the North American continent; its continental

range extends from Labrador to Alaska and south to Pennsylvania, Ohio and Washington. Its leaves have from time to time been used as a substitute for tea. (Bog-tea.) The flowers are shown on Pl. 19, 5; the foliage and fruit on p. 117, a.

(2)   **Lapland Rosebay**   *Rhododendron lapponicum* (L.) Wahlenb. The Lapland rosebay grows prostrate on the ground instead of erect. The flowers appear early in the season and are bell-shaped and regular, and pink-magenta in color. The leaves are narrow, leathery and evergreen, and the whole plant is covered with rusty scales or dots. It is a circumpolar species in the Arctic and subarctic; in North America it extends south to Katahdin, the White Mountains and the Adirondacks, and to the Dells of the Wisconsin River in Wisconsin. The plants are shown on Pl. 21, 2 and 22, 1 and 3.

(3)   **Rhodora**   *Rhododendron canadense* (L.) Torr. Rhodora is one of relatively few of our heaths with deciduous leaves. The flowers open early in the spring before the leaves have expanded. The pinkish flush that rhodora imparts to a bog is more generally noticed than the detail of the individual blossoms. The blossoms, while tubular as are those of most heaths, are deeply cleft, irregular, and consist of a three-toothed lip and two narrow, strap-shaped segments. The leaves are not so thick as those of Labrador tea, and while covered with a short down they are not woolly. The species is found in bogs and on barren summits from Newfoundland to northeastern Pennsylvania and west to northern New York. The plant is shown on Pl. 19, 3; the flowers and fruit on p. 117, b.

(4)   **Alpine Azalea**   *Loiseleuria procumbens* (L.) Desv. The alpine azalea is far less conspicuous than the azaleas of the garden which belong to the genus *Rhododendron*. The alpine azalea is low and somewhat moss-like, with small, leathery, evergreen leaves. The flowers are only about $\frac{1}{4}$ inch long, they are bell-shaped, and pink to somewhat rose-colored. The genus is named in honor of Loiseleur-Delongchamps, a French botanist. A number of other heaths are also named for botanists or scientists in other fields. *Kalmia* is named for Peter Kalm, a student of Linnaeus who traveled and collected plants in North America, and the huckleberry, *Gaylussacia*, is named for Gay-Lussac, the French chemist. The species is a circumpolar arctic-alpine plant; in eastern North America it extends south to the high mountains of Maine and New Hampshire. The flowers are shown on Pl. 20, 4; the plants on 21, 2 and 3.

(5)   **Sheep Laurel**   *Kalmia angustifolia* L. The two laurels considered here have rather similar blossoms but the inflorescence in this species is lateral on the branch while that of the pale laurel is terminal. The leaves are opposite or in whorls of three, the blades are flat, and a short stalk connects the blade to the twig. Sheep laurel is a common shrub in our area in bogs and old pastures and it is frequently found on ledges near the tops of our lower mountains. The species is found from Labrador to Manitoba and south in the mountains to Georgia. The leaves of both laurels are quite poisonous to livestock when eaten, hence the names sheep laurel and lambkill. (Pig-laurel, dwarf laurel, wicky.) The foliage and flowers are shown on Pl. 23, 2.

(6)   **Pale Laurel**   *Kalmia polifolia* Wang. The pale laurel is a more slender shrub than the previous species. The flowers are usually a paler color, a trifle larger and somewhat fewer in the inflorescence. The leaves are narrower, the margins are inrolled and the blades grow directly from the twigs. The pale laurel is found in peaty soils from Labrador to Alaska and south to Pennsylvania, Wyoming and California. (Bog-laurel.) The foliage and flowers are shown on Pl. 23, 1.

(7)   **Mountain Heath**   *Phyllodoce caerulea* (L.) Bab. The lavender, urn-shaped, nodding flowers of the mountain heath are very conspicuous in the early part of the season, particularly around late-melting snowbanks. While the blossoms are shaped somewhat like those of the true heath of Europe, the plants of *Phyllodoce* are shorter and more moss-like. The species is a circumboreal subarctic-alpine which extends south in eastern North America to the high mountains of Maine and New Hampshire. A number of related species are found in the mountains of the West. The generic name is that of a Roman sea-nymph. Several other heaths also have generic names derived from classical mythology; these include *Cassiope* and her daughter *Andromeda* as well as *Leucothoë* and *Cassandra*. A plant is shown on Pl. 22, 4.

(8)   **Bog-Rosemary**   *Andromeda glaucophylla* Link. In our area the bog-rosemary is a characteristic plant of cold bogs. It is a low shrub with narrow leaves which have inrolled margins and the under surface covered with minute white hairs. The turban-shaped flowers are white or pink. The species is found from Labrador to Manitoba and south to West Virginia and Indiana. It is not an alpine plant but it sometimes occurs in bogs well up on the mountains. A flowering branch is shown on p. 117, c.

(9)   **Leather-leaf** *Chamaedaphne   calyculata*   (L.)   Moench.
Leather-leaf is another characteristic shrub of bogs. The leaves
are evergreen, flat and scurfy, particularly on the under surface.
The flowers are cylindric and white. The species is Eurasian. Two
varieties occur in North America. Var. *angustifolia* (Ait.) Rehd.
is the common lowland variety. The leaves are about one-fourth
as broad as long and the sepals are sharp-pointed. This variety
occurs in eastern Asia and from Newfoundland to Alaska and south
to Georgia and Ohio. Var. *latifolia* (Ait.) Fern. has leaves which
are one-half as broad as long, and blunt sepals. It is more northern in its range extending from Labrador to the Mackenzie and
south to northern New England. Typical specimens of the two
varieties are quite distinct but there are many plants which are
intermediate in their characters. (Cassandra.) A flowering branch
of var. *angustifolia* and a single leaf of var. *latifolia* are shown
on p. 117, d.

(10)   **Moss Plant**   *Cassiope hypnoides* (L.) D. Don. The moss
plant is well named. Its small size coupled with its nodding white
flowers make it one of the daintiest and most attractive of the alpine
heaths. Unless seen in flower almost anyone might mistake it for
a moss or fail to notice it at all. It is found in northern Eurasia and
from Greenland to Labrador and south to Katahdin and the Presidential Range. While Cassiope's treatment of Perseus hardly makes
her worthy of being honored by such a dainty plant I still feel that
the name is preferable to *Harrimanella* which is used by some botanists for the genus. The plant is shown on Pl. 22, 2 and 23, 4.

(11)   **Creeping Snowberry**   *Gaultheria hispidula* (L.) Bigel. The
creeping snowberry bears little resemblance to its sister species in
our area, *G. procumbens*, the checkerberry. The snowberry is a
prostrate plant with small broad leaves which are ciliate. The
flowers are inconspicuous; the berries are white and have a slight
wintergreen flavor. It is a common plant in cool, mossy, coniferous
woods and it ascends the mountains to the krummholz near timberline. Its range extends from Labrador to British Columbia and
south to the uplands of North Carolina and Idaho. (Moxie-plum,
Maidenhair-berry.) A fruiting plant is shown on Pl. 23, 6.

(12)   **Alpine Bearberry**   *Arctostaphylos alpina* (L.) Spreng. I
have never been lucky enough to find the alpine bearberry in flower
or fruit but the foliage alone is ample for a sure identification. The
leaves are deciduous, the margins are slightly toothed and the veins
strongly developed giving a wrinkled appearance to the blade. In
the fall they turn a deep red color. The yellowish-green flowers

a. **Labrador Tea**
   Ledum groenlandicum

b. **Rhodora**
   Rhododendron canadense

c. **Bog-Rosemary**
   Andromeda glaucophylla

d. **Leather-leaf**
   Chamaedaphne calyculata, var. *angustifolia* leaf var. *latifolia*

e. **Dwarf Bilberry**
   Vaccinium caespitosum

f. **Velvet-leaf Blueberry**
   Vaccinium myrtilloides

appear in the spring before the leaves expand. The berries are black. It is a circumpolar subarctic species which extends south to Newfoundland, eastern Quebec, Katahdin and the Presidential Range. In our lowlands the bearberry, *A. Uva-ursi*, is found on exposed rocks and sand. In the West the genus is represented by a formidable group of taller species which are known as Manzanitas. (Poisonberry.) A fruiting plant is shown on Pl. 23, 5.

(13)   **Bog Bilberry**   *Vaccinium uliginosum* L., var. *alpinum* Bigel. The bilberries look and taste much like blueberries, but the two differ in a number of characteristics. The flowers and fruit are axillary in bilberries and are borne singly or in twos and threes; the berries are four- to five-celled; and the stamens have glabrous filaments and a pair of horn-like awns on the anthers. The bog bilberry has broad, entire leaves, four-parted flowers, and dark blue to black berries. The species is circumpolar; the variety extends south from the Arctic to the mountains of New England and New York and to northern Michigan and northern Minnesota. The flowers are shown on Pl. 24, 1; the fruit on 24, 2.

(14)   **Dwarf bilberry**   *Vaccinium cespitosum* Michx. The dwarf bilberry is a lower plant, the leaves are broadest above the middle and have toothed margins, the flowers and fruit are five-parted, and the berries are light blue. The dwarf bilberry is found from Labrador to Alaska and south to northern New England and New York, to Colorado and California. A fruiting branch is shown on p. 117, e.

(15)   **Velvet-leaf Blueberry**   *Vaccinium myrtilloides* Michx. In the true blueberries the flowers and fruit are terminal instead of axillary, and they occur in groups of more than three; the berries are eight- to ten-celled; the anthers of the stamens lack awns and the filaments are hairy. In the velvet-leaf blueberry the young branchlets and at least the undersurfaces of the leaves are hairy, the margins of the leaves are not toothed, and the berries are covered with a heavy bloom. Its range extends from Newfoundland to British Columbia and south to the mountains of Virginia, to Iowa and Montana. The species is common in the lowlands of our area and it is occasional on mountain tops and in alpine ravines. (Sour-top blueberry.) Autumn foliage is shown on Pl. 25, 1; flowers and fruit on p. 117, f.

(16)   **Low Sweet Blueberry**   *Vaccinium angustifolium* Ait. The low sweet blueberry is not conspicuously hairy, the margins of the leaves are finely toothed, and the berries are bright blue. A number

of varieties are recognized. The dwarf alpine plants belong to var. *angustifolium*. Var. *laevifolium* House is a taller plant with broader leaves and larger flowers. This variety is the common low-bush blueberry of our lowlands and it may occur near the summits of our lower mountains. Var. *angustifolium* is found from Labrador to Minnesota and south to the mountains of New England and New York. The range of var. *laevifolium* extends from Newfoundland to Saskatchewan and south to West Virginia and Iowa. (Late sweet blueberry, sweet hurts.) Flowering plants are shown on Pl. 23, 3.

(17) **Mountain Cranberry** *Vaccinium Vitis-Idaea* L., var. *minus* Lodd. The mountain cranberry is widespread in the subarctic of both hemispheres. It extends south to the mountains of New England but not New York, and also down the coast of Maine. An isolated station existed in Danvers, Massachusetts, but this colony is probably now extinct. While the berries are somewhat slow to pick they are well worth the effort for they make excellent sauce or jelly, having a wild flavor lacking in the cultivated cranberry. Prof. M. L. Fernald has pointed out that the wineberry mentioned by the Norsemen in the sagas describing the discovery of Vineland is probably the mountain cranberry with which the Norsemen were well acquainted, rather than the grape as is generally supposed. (Cowberry, partridgeberry, red-whortleberry.) Flowers are shown on Pl. 24, 3; fruit on 24, 4.

(18) **Wren's Egg Cranberry** *Vaccinium Oxycoccos* L. The name "wren's egg cranberry" is applied to this plant by the natives on some of the islands along the Maine coast because the unripe berries are spotted like a bird's egg. The plant is a miniature edition of the cultivated cranberry. Both are trailing vines and both have nodding flowers with four almost separate, reflexed petals looking much like the flowers of the shooting star. It is a circumboreal species which extends as far south as North Carolina in the East and Oregon in the West. It is a plant of cold bogs at lower elevations in our area and it occasionally occurs at elevations of up to 5000 feet on our mountains. (Small cranberry.) Flowers are shown on Pl. 24, 5; fruit on 24, 6.

DIAPENSIACEAE (Diapensia Family)

This is a small family of six genera which differs from the heaths in having the stamens attached to the corolla tube. In addition to the circumboreal *Diapensia* the family includes the pixie moss of the New Jersey pine barrens, the very local *Shortia* of the southeastern states, and *Galax*, also southeastern, whose leaves garnish Memorial Day wreaths and bunches of hothouse violets.

Diapensia *Diapensia lapponica* L. Although the erect white flowers of diapensia are very conspicuous, they open so early in the season that they are missed by most climbers. However, the cushion-like tufts of bright green foliage are characteristic of the rather barren ground above treeline. The species is a circumpolar subarctic-alpine which extends south to the higher mountains of our area. Plants are shown on Pl. 21, 2; flowers on 26, 3.

PRIMULACEAE (Primrose Family)

The primrose family has relatively few species in this area, the most conspicuous being the loosestrifes. The number of floral parts varies but five is the most common number. The leaves are simple and either opposite or whorled. The shooting-star and the cultivated primulas and cyclamens also belong to this family.

Star Flower *Trientalis borealis* Raf. The star flower is the only member of the primrose family to be found above timberline in our area; it is a common woodland flower at lower elevations. The narrow, lance-shaped leaves are grouped in a whorl at the top of a short stem. The white flowers are not large but are distinctive in usually having the parts in sevens, not a common condition. While the petals are united at their bases, they are flat and spreading and there is little indication of a tube. The species has a range which extends from Labrador to Alberta and south to West Virginia and Minnesota. In the West there are a number of similar species. (Chickweed-wintergreen.) Enlarged flowers are shown on Pl. 26, 1; a plant on 26, 2.

GENTIANACEAE (Gentian Family)

The members of this family have simple entire leaves which are opposite or whorled; the flowers have a plan of four or five and in some genera are quite showy. Most of the species are herbs. One of our lowland species is an aquatic with floating leaves which resemble small water lily leaves. None of the species of our area, with the possible exception of the floating-heart, is really common.

Closed Gentian *Gentiana linearis* Froel. The alpine areas of our region lack the gentians characteristic of the Alps and the mountains of the West. *G. linearis* occurs at lower elevations in our region. It is a fairly tall plant with narrow opposite leaves. The flowers appear in mid-summer and are cylindrical and of a rich porcelain-blue color. The species is found from Labrador to Minnesota and south to West Virginia. The plant is found in damp openings high up on Mt. Marcy and might be found in similar habitats on our other mountains. Flowers and foliage are shown on Pl. 26, 5.

Labiatae (Mint Family)

The mints make up a large family of plants of world-wide distribution. In our area they are chiefly herbs with four-sided stems and opposite simple leaves which contain aromatic oils. The flowers tend to be two-lipped and the fruits are four seed-like nutlets. Many species occur in our area either as native plants or as introduced weeds.

Self-heal   *Prunella vulgaris* L., var. *lanceolata* (Bart.) Fern. Self-heal or heal-all is a common flower of fields and woods over much of the United States and Canada. It is the only member of the Mint Family that one is likely to encounter above treeline. The stem is square in cross-section, as in most mints, and the leaves are opposite. The purple to flesh-colored flowers grow in a terminal spike. The blossoms are arranged in three-flowered clusters, half-hidden by round floral leaves. The common name dates back to the days of the herbalists, who believed that the plant had medicinal value in treating a disease of the throat. The species is native to Eurasia. The variety occurs in eastern Asia and the northern parts of North America. Self-heal is occasionally found above or close to treeline; whether it is native there or has been introduced from lower elevations is a matter of doubt. An inflorescence is shown on Pl. 25, 4.

Scrophulariaceae (Figwort Family)

The figworts make up another large family found all over the world. The plants are mostly herbaceous and have simple leaves; the flowers are usually two-lipped and have two or four functional stamens. The fruit is a capsule containing many seeds. There are many native and introduced species in our region such as mullein, butter-and-eggs, monkey-flower, foxglove and wood-betony.

1. Leaves opposite . . . . 2.
1. Leaves alternate; tall plants with terminal spikes of cream-colored flowers   (3) **Pale Painted Cup** *Castilleja septentrionalis*
    2. Plants less than 5 inches tall; flowers inconspicuous, al-

121

most hidden under floral bracts . . . . 3.

2. Plants often more than 5 inches tall; flowers more conspicuous . . . . 4.

3. Flowers whitish; leaves smaller than the floral bracts, pubescent, sinuses between teeth rounded

(5) **Eyebright** *Euphrasia Oakesii*

3. Flowers brownish-purple; leaves the same size as the floral bracts, smooth or somewhat pubescent, sinuses between teeth acute (6) **Eyebright** *Euphrasia Williamsii*

4. Flowers in a terminal head . . . . 5.

4. Flowers axillary; leaves narrow with few if any teeth

(4) **Cow-wheat** *Melampyrum lineare*

5. Flowers blue, flat and wheel-shaped; leaves elliptical or rounded, distinctly hairy (2) **Alpine Speedwell** *Veronica alpina*

5. Flowers white or yellow, tubular and hooded; leaves distinctly toothed, smooth or nearly so . . . . 6.

6. Flowers white, calyx much shorter than corolla, not inflated (1) **Turtlehead** *Chelone glabra*

6. Flowers yellow, calyx inflated and at least half as long as the corolla (7) **Yellow Rattle** *Rhinanthus borealis*

(1) **Turtlehead** *Chelone glabra* L. The turtlehead is a relatively tall plant of damp ground in our area. The leaves are more or less lance-shaped with distinct teeth; the blossoms are white and an inch or more long. The species occurs from Newfoundland to Ontario and south to Georgia and Missouri. It is not an alpine species but it does occasionally occur in wooded swamps well up on the mountains. (Snakehead, balmony.) A flowering stem is shown on p. 123, a.

(2) **Alpine Speedwell** *Veronica alpina* L., var. *unalaschcensis* C. & S. The alpine speedwell, or mountain forget-me-not, looks superficially like the true forget-me-nots, although they are only distantly related. The stems are relatively low, the leaves are opposite, and the entire plant is hairy. The small blue flowers are wheel-shaped rather than being hooded as in most members of the Figwort Family. The species is a circumpolar arctic one; the variety occurs from Greenland to Alaska and south to the mountains of New England and Colorado. In our area the alpine speedwell is found along the streams in alpine ravines on Katahdin and Mt. Washington. Flowers are shown on Pl. 25, 2.

(3) **Pale Painted Cup** *Castilleja septentrionalis* Lindl. The painted cups, like certain other members of the Figwort Family,

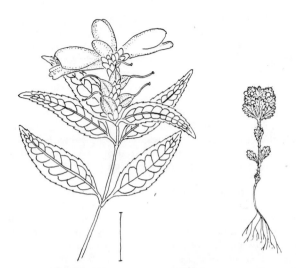

a. **Turtlehead**
Chelone glabra

b. **Eyebright**
Euphrasia Oakesii

are root parasites on other plants. In the West there are numerous species which are very difficult to separate. On our mountains identification is easy because we have only one species to contend with. It is a plant of medium height with alternate, lance-shaped leaves which are usually untoothed. The flowers are in a terminal spike, and the blossoms themselves are less conspicuous than the cream-colored to purplish floral leaves behind which they are hidden. The species occurs from Labrador to Alberta and south to the mountains of New England and Colorado. In our area the plant is found on the heads of subalpine ravines on Katahdin and Mt. Washington and in the notches of northern Vermont. An inflorescence is shown on Pl. 25, 3.

(4) **Cow-wheat** *Melampyrum lineare* Desr. The cow-wheat is a slender annual with narrow lance-shaped leaves and small axillary white flowers. A number of varieties are recognized. The plants found above timberline belong to var. *lineare* which has a range extending from Labrador to British Columbia and south to the mountains of New England and Idaho. Var. *americanum* (Michx.) Beauverd, which is more branching and has somewhat broader leaves and toothed floral leaves, is fairly common in our area at lower elevations. A flowering stem is shown on Pl. 27, 1.

123

(5)   **Eyebright** *Euphrasia Oakesii* Wettst. The eyebrights are among the smallest of the flowering plants here treated, the stems often being about two inches high. Like the painted cup they are root parasites. The leaves are opposite, nearly round and toothed. The sinuses between the teeth are rounded and both surfaces of the blades are hairy. The flowers are in a terminal spike, and are small and white, almost hidden by the floral leaves which are larger than the stem leaves. The species is found in Labrador, Newfoundland, and the Gaspé Peninsula, and on Katahdin and Mt. Washington. While the name "eyebright" was given the genus because of its former use in diseases of the eye, it also suggests the difficulty of finding the species. A plant is shown on p. 123, b.

(6)   **Eyebright** *Euphrasia Williamsii* Robins. This species is very similar to the previous one. It differs in the flowers being brownish-red, in having the floral and stem leaves about the same size, the leaf blades glabrous or only slightly hairy, and the sinuses between the teeth being acute instead of rounded. The range of this species is also similar but more restricted; it occurs in Newfoundland, the Gaspé Peninsula and Mt. Washington. A variety is found in northern and western Newfoundland and adjacent Quebec. Plants are shown on Pl. 28, 2 and 29, 1.

(7)   **Yellow Rattle** *Rhinanthus borealis* (Sterneck) Chabert. The yellow rattle is an annual of medium height. The leaves are opposite, somewhat oblong in shape, and conspicuously toothed. The two to twelve yellow flowers are in a one-sided, leafy spike, the floral leaves being triangular in outline and taper-pointed. The calyx of the blossom, after the flowering period, becomes inflated and almost spherical. The species is found in Greenland and arctic America and south to the mountains of New England and New York. A very similar species, *R. Crista-galli*, is found near the coast from Newfoundland to New England. An inflorescence is shown on Pl. 27, 2.

RUBIACEAE (Madder Family)

The madder family is a large family found chiefly in tropical and subtropical regions where coffee, *Coffea*, and the source of quinine, *Cinchona*, are its most important members. The entire leaves are opposite or whorled; the flowers are four- or five-parted and regular; the fruits are various; among our native genera the bluets have capsules, the bedstraws two dry subglobose carpels, and the partridgeberry berries.

124

Alpine Bluet *Houstonia caerulea* L., var. *Faxonorum* Pease & Moore. Most readers are familiar with the common bluet. The name bluet is a misnomer for the variety *Faxonorum* since the blossoms are white. This variety is a somewhat more robust plant than the typical one, the seeds are also somewhat larger. It was named in honor of Edwin and Charles Edward Faxon, brothers who collected extensively in the White Mountains. The alpine bluet is known only from the White Mountains and the islands of St. Pierre and Miquelon off Newfoundland. In the spring the bluet forms large mats on the alpine meadows of Mt. Washington. The common bluet, var. *caerulea*, also may occasionally be found fairly well up on our mountains. Flowers are shown on Pl. 26, 4.

CAPRIFOLIACEAE (Honeysuckle Family)

This family is most abundant in the temperate parts of the Northern Hemisphere, reaching its highest development in eastern North America. Most of its members have woody stems; the leaves are opposite and simple in most genera; the flowers are either regular or bilaterally symmetrical; the fruits are drupes or berries. The family is well represented in our area and various honeysuckles and viburnums are common cultivated shrubs and vines.

1. Flowers yellow or yellowish . . . . 2.
1. Flowers white . . . . 3.
   2. Leaves toothed; flowers borne in threes; fruit a capsule
            (1) **Bush Honeysuckle** *Diervilla Lonicera*
   2. Leaves entire; flowers borne in pairs; fruit a berry
        (2) **Mountain Fly Honeysuckle** *Lonicera villosa*
3. Creeping vines with evergreen leaves; flowers borne in pairs, nodding and bell-shaped   (3) **Twinflower** *Linnaea borealis*
3. Not creeping vines; leaves not evergreen . . . . 4.
   4. Leaves simple . . . . 5.
   4. Leaves compound (7) **Red-berried Elder** *Sambucus pubens*
5. Marginal flowers large, flat and neutral; leaf outline nearly circular   (4) **Hobblebush** *Viburnum alnifolium*
5. Flowers all similar; leaves not circular . . . . 6.
   6. Leaves unlobed, tapering to apex and base; fruits blue-black when ripe   (5) **Wild raisin** *Viburnum cassinoides*
   6. Leaves usually three-lobed, not tapering to base; ripe fruits red   (6) **Squashberry** *Viburnum edule*

(1)   **Bush Honeysuckle** *Diervilla Lonicera* Mill. The bush honeysuckle is a common shrub in the woods of our area, and it sometimes reaches the upper limit of the trees. The oval leaves are

taper-pointed, toothed, and opposite in their arrangement. The flower clusters are terminal, the flowers being borne in groups of three. The yellow blossoms are funnel-shaped and have five similar lobes. The fruits are long-beaked pods. The species extends from Newfoundland to Manitoba and southward to the mountains of North Carolina. A flowering branch is shown on p. 127, d.

(2)   **Mountain Fly Honeysuckle**   *Lonicera villosa* (Michx.) R. & S. The mountain fly honeysuckle is fairly common above treeline. The oblong leaves are entire; the yellow flowers are borne in pairs; and the two ovaries unite in the fruit to form a single blue berry, which is edible. The shrub blooms in late June. Four varieties are recognized which occur in our area, but many intermediate plants are also found. Var. *villosa* has densely hairy leaves and hairs of two lengths on the branchlets; the calyx and corolla are also hairy. The calyx and corolla are smooth in the following three varieties. In var. *Solonis* (Eat.) Fern. the leaves may be hairy on both sur-faces and the branchlets bear hairs of two lengths. Var. *calvescens* (Fern. & Wieg.) Fern. has only short hairs on the branchlets and the under surfaces of the leaves may be smooth. In var. *tonsa* Fern. the branchlets and usually the leaves are smooth. The total range of the varieties extends from Labrador to Manitoba and south to Pennsylvania and Minnesota. (Waterberry.) A flowering plant is shown on Pl. 27, 3, and flowers and fruit on p. 127, e.

(3)   **Twinflower**   *Linnaea borealis* L., var. *americana* (Forbes) Rehd. The twinflower is a dainty creeping evergreen of the north-ern woods of both the Old World and the New. It was a favorite plant of Linnaeus, who is often pictured holding a sprig of it in his hand; it was named in his honor by Gronovius. The leaves are nearly round, with a few teeth. Each slender upright stem forks into two at the top, and each fork bears a nodding, bell-shaped, whitish to somewhat pinkish flower. Its delicious fragrance is often the first indication of the twinflower's presence. It is one of the loveliest of our woodland flowers at lower elevations and it often extends well up into the krummholz. Flowers are shown on Pl. 26, 6; a portion of a plant on p. 127, c.

(4)   **Hobblebush**   *Viburnum alnifolium* Marsh. The hobblebush does not extend much above 3000 feet on our mountains but it is a conspicuous shrub on the lower slopes. The leaves are large and almost circular. The inflorescences are showy in the early summer, the marginal flowers being sterile and nearly an inch in diameter. Later in the season the fruits are bright red, finally darkening to nearly black. Hobblebush is found from Prince Edward Island to

a. **Red-berried Elder**
   Sambucus pubens

b. **Wild Raisin**
   Viburnum cassinoides

c. **Twinflower**
   Linnaea borealis,
   var. *americana*

d. **Bush Honeysuckle**
   Diervilla Lonicera

e. **Mountain Fly Honeysuckle**
   Lonicera villosa

Ontario and south to the mountains of Georgia and Tennessee. (Witch-hobble, tangle-legs, she-moosewood, wayfaring tree.) A flowering branch is shown on Pl. 28, 4.

(5)   **Wild Raisin**   *Viburnum cassinoides* L. The wild raisin is another common shrub at lower elevations which occasionally is found well up on our mountains. The leaves are broadest near the middle and taper to each end; the flowers are small and all alike. The fruits are yellow at first, later pink, and finally blue-black. The mature fruits have a sweet pulp which is quite palatable but the large flat stones get in the way. *V. cassinoides* is found from New-

foundland to Manitoba and south to Alabama. (Witherod, sheepberry, Appalachian-tea.) A branch showing flowers and fruit is shown on p. 127, b.

(6)   **Squashberry**   *Viburnum edule* (Michx.) Raf. The squashberry is a low shrub which makes its way above the timber on the mountains of our area. The leaf is usually three-lobed and somewhat maple-like; the flowers are small and white; the fruits are red when ripe. The acid pulp is sometimes used as a substitute for cranberries. The plant is found in cool woods from Labrador to Alaska and south to Pennsylvania, Colorado and Oregon. (Mooseberry, pimbina.) A flowering stem is shown on Pl. 27, 4.

(7)   **Red-berried Elder**   *Sambucus pubens* Michx. The red-berried or stinking elder is rather similar to the common elder of our area. It differs in having brown pith in the twigs, in blooming earlier in the season, and in having red berries. The leaves are compound with five to seven leaflets. It is a plant of cool woods from Newfoundland to Alaska and south to the mountains of Georgia, Colorado, and Oregon. While not an alpine plant it does reach the summits of the lower mountains of our area and into some of the alpine ravines. The berries are inedible. (Stinking elder.) A fruiting branch is shown on p. 127, a.

CAMPANULACEAE (Bluebell Family)

In our area the members of this family are herbs with alternate leaves and flowers which are regular or bilaterally symmetrical. The fruits are capsules. The number of species in our region is not large; in addition to the bluebells we have the cardinal-flower and a few lobelias.

Bluebell   *Campanula rotundifolia* L. It seems surprising that a plant which appears as delicate as the bluebell can survive above timberline, yet there it is. The specific name *rotundifolia* may seem a misnomer, for the stem leaves are narrow and somewhat lance-shaped. The name applies to the basal leaves, which are rounded and somewhat heart-shaped. At lower altitudes the bluebell grows to be a foot or more tall, and the stem bears several blossoms. Above timberline the plants are seldom over 6 inches tall and usually bear a single flower. This dwarfed form has been segregated as the dubious variety *arctica* Lange. The species is circumboreal in its distribution and it is found over much of the United States. Plants and flowers are shown on Pl. 28, 1 and 3.

COMPOSITAE (Composite Family)

The composite family is the largest family of flowering plants containing nearly a thousand genera and twenty times as many species. The composites differ from the other families of flowering plants in the structure of the blossoms. At first glance a daisy may seem to be a single flower; actually it is more like a bunch of flowers enclosed in a ring of leaves. In the daisy, however, the flowers are of two sorts; there is an outer ring of white, petal-like *ray flowers*, and a central portion made up of a large number of yellow *disk flowers*. The disk to which both sorts of flowers are attached is called the *receptacle*. The flowers are enclosed by the green, cup-shaped *involucre* made up of a varying number of scale-like *involucral bracts*. The seed-like fruits of composites are achenes. The summit of the achenes of most of the species treated here is crowned by a ring of long, often feathery, bristles which make up the *pappus*. The relative positions of the parts mentioned are illustrated in the accompanying diagram.

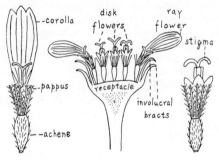

Many of our familiar plants, both wild and cultivated, belong to this family. Among the wild ones are the goldenrods, asters, ragweeds, daisies, thistles, dandelions and hawkweeds. Included in the cultivated forms are the sunflowers, cosmos, gaillardia, marigolds, dahlias, and zinnias, as well as a number of vegetables such as lettuce, endive and both the French and Jerusalem artichokes. The last-named plant is a good example of how common names may lead one astray, the plant being native to Mexico and the name "Jerusalem" a corruption of "Girasol," the Spanish word for sunflower.

In our area the composites reach their peak about midsummer and continue to be conspicuous well into the fall. Large genera such as the goldenrods and asters present problems in identification because hybridization is frequent, resulting in numerous plants which seem to be intermediate between two species. Fortunately the number of species one is likely to encounter above timberline is not large.

1. Heads with yellow ray flowers . . . . 2.
1. Ray flowers not yellow, or wanting . . . . 5.
   2. Heads relatively small and numerous; leaves alternate (goldenrods) . . . . 3.
   2. Heads large and few; leaves mostly opposite
                              (12) **Arnica** *Arnica mollis*
3. Small plants usually not more than 6 inches tall; stem leaves four or five   (2) **Alpine Goldenrod** *Solidago Cutleri*
3. Plants with stout stems, often a foot or more tall; stem leaves numerous . . . . 4.
   4. Stem leaves thin, broadest near or below the middle, tapering abruptly into winged petioles (stalks); heads ½ inch or more high
       (1) **Large-leaved Goldenrod** *Solidago macrophylla*
   4. Stem leaves thicker and smaller, much reduced upwards, broadest above the middle, tapering gradually into winged petioles; heads about ¼ inch high
           (3) **Rand's Goldenrod** *Solidago Randii*
5. Plants white, woolly or silky   . . . . 6.
5. Plants not white, woolly . . . . 8.
   6. Both ray and disk flowers present; leaves finely dissected   (11) **Yarrow** *Achillea borealis*
   6. Only disk flowers present; leaves entire . . . . 7.
7. Tall plants with numerous stem leaves; heads with conspicuous white involucral bracts
      (9) **Pearly Everlasting** *Anaphalis margaritacea*
7. Dwarf plants; leaves mostly basal; heads inconspicuous
      (10) **Mountain Cudweed** *Gnaphalium supinum*
   8. Heads with both ray and disk flowers; involucral bracts in a number of rows (asters) . . . . 9.
   8. Heads with only ray flowers; involucral bracts in a single row . . . . 13.
9. Rays blue, violet or lilac . . . . 10.
9. Rays white . . . . 12.
   10. Leaf bases broad and somewhat clasping . . . . . . 11.
   10. Leaves tapering to base and apex, bases not clasping
         (5) **Rough-bracted Aster** *Aster radula*
11. Stems hairy; leaves distinctly toothed; heads large
         (4) **Purple-stem Aster** *Aster puniceus*
11. Stems not conspicuously hairy; leaves slightly if at all

toothed; heads smaller
> (6) **Leafy-bracted Aster** *Aster foliaceous*

12. Leaves distinctly toothed; relatively low plants
> (7) **Sharp-leaved Wood Aster** *Aster acuminatus*

12. Leaves entire, numerous; tall plant
> (8) **Umbellate Aster** *Aster umbellatus*

13. Heads eight- to eighteen-flowered; involucral bracts seven
to ten . . . . 14.

13. Heads five- to six-flowered; involucral bracts usually five
> (14) **Tall Rattlesnake-root** *Prenanthes altissima*

14. Lower leaves deeply lobed; heads eight- to twelve-flowered   (13) **Low Rattlesnake-root** *Prenanthes trifoliolata*

14. Lower leaves entire or somewhat toothed; heads ten- to
eighteen-flowered
> (15) **Boott's Rattlesnake-root** *Prenanthes Boottii*

(1)   **Large-leaved Goldenrod** *Solidago macrophylla* Pursh. The goldenrods in the lowlands are confusing because of the number of species involved. The situation is simplified above treeline because only three species are likely to be encountered. Of these *S. macrophylla* is the stoutest. As the name implies, the leaves are large, the blades of some of the lower ones being 4 inches long and about 3 wide. The blade tapers into the leaf-stalk or petiole. The edges of the blade are closely toothed, and the blade is thin in texture. Var. *macrophylla* occurs from Labrador to Ontario and south to Massachusetts and New York. It is a tall plant; the largest terminal heads contain up to about thirty flowers. This variety is found in cool lowland woods of our area and on the lower summits. On Katahdin and the White Mountains var. *thyrsoidea* (Mey.) Fern. is also found. This is a lower plant with very large heads that contain up to one hundred flowers. Its range extends from our area north to Labrador and Ungava. An inflorescence is shown on Pl. 29, 3.

(2)   **Alpine Goldenrod** *Solidago Cutleri* Fern. This is the smallest of the alpine goldenrods, seldom being as much as 10 inches tall. The leaves are thicker than those of the previous species, and the stem bears not more than five leaves. The leaves are broadest above the middle and are all of about the same size. The inflorescence is made up of relatively few heads, which are somewhat bell-shaped, about $\frac{1}{4}$ inch high and many flowered. The species was named for the Reverend Manasseh Cutler, an early New England botanist, who visited Mt. Washington in 1784 and again in 1804. The Cutler River on Mt. Washington is also named

in his honor. The species is confined to the highest summits of our area. A plant is shown on Pl. 29, 4.

(3) **Rand's Goldenrod** *Solidago Randii* (Porter) Britt. This is a fairly tall species, but the stems are not so stout as those of *S. macrophylla* and they are often tinged with purple. The leaves are smaller and thicker, and taper more gradually into the petiole. The upper stem leaves are much smaller than the lower ones. The heads are about $\frac{1}{4}$ inch high, and in the plants found above timberline the heads are aggregated into a cylindrical inflorescence. The species is named for Edward L. Rand, an enthusiastic amateur botanist and one of the authors of the *Flora of Mount Desert Island.* The species is found from Nova Scotia to Lake Superior and south to northern New England and New York. It is not an alpine but it does occur above timberline. A plant is shown on p. 133, a.

(4) **Purple-stem Aster** *Aster puniceus* L. The purple-stem aster is a relatively tall stout species; the lower portion of the stem is purple and the upper portion is covered with coarse, harsh, white hairs. The leaves are lance-shaped with rounded bases which clasp the stem; the upper surfaces of the leaves are often rough to the touch. The stem bears relatively few large heads. The species is found from Newfoundland to Saskatchewan and south to Alabama and Georgia. A number of varieties are recognized. The alpine plants are likely to be var. *oligocephalus* Fern., which is lower and stouter than the typical variety and has leafy bracts surrounding the one or two large heads. A flowering stem is shown on p. 133, b.

(5) **Rough-dracted Aster** *Aster radula* Ait. In *A. radula* the leaves taper to either end, the margins are sharply toothed, and the upper surface or both surfaces are harsh to the touch. The involucral bracts of the head often have recurved tips which are the source of the specific name *radula* meaning scraper. The species is found in low woods and bogs from Newfoundland and Quebec to Virginia. While usually a lowland species it occasionally is found in bogs on the mountains at elevations of up to 4500 feet. The slender, few-headed plants found in such localities are segregated by some botanists as variety *strictus* (Pursh) Gray. Flowers are shown on Pl. 28, 5; a flowering stem on p. 133, c.

(6) **Leafy-bracted Aster** *Aster foliaceus* L. This species has clasping leaves like those of *A. puniceus* but the margins have few if any teeth. The stem is green, slender, and smooth except for some short hairs on the upper portion. The heads are few in number; the outer series of involucral bracts are broad and leaf-like.

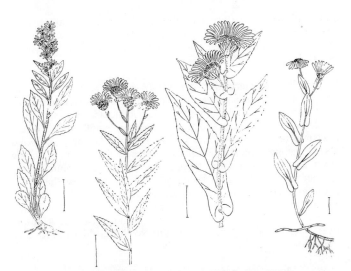

a. **Rand's Goldenrod**
   Solidago Randii

b. **Purple-stem Aster**
   Aster puniceus

c. **Rough-bracted Aster**
   Aster radula

d. **Leafy-bracted Aster**
   Aster foliaceus

The species is found from Labrador and eastern Quebec to the mountains of northern New England; it also occurs in the Far West. This is the most common blue-flowered aster found above treeline in our mountains. While fairly easy to recognize, its taxonomic status, like that of many other asters, is still a matter of debate. A plant is shown on p. 133, d.

(7)   **Sharp-leaved Wood Aster**   *Aster acuminatus* Michx. This species is common in the open woods of our area and it frequently ascends to wooded mountain tops. The large, coarsely toothed leaves taper to both ends and often form a spreading cluster beneath the inflorescence. The heads are usually relatively few in number; the ray flowers are long and slender and are usually white. The species is found from southwestern Newfoundland to Ontario and south to the mountains of Georgia. A flowering plant is shown on Pl. 30, 2.

(8)   **Umbellate Aster**   *Aster umbellatus* Mill. *A. umbellatus* is a fairly tall species with many narrow entire leaves. The heads are very numerous and form a broad, flat-topped inflorescence. It is a plant of thickets and meadows from Newfoundland to Ontario

and south to North Carolina and Georgia. While usually a lowland species it is occasionally found at elevations up to 5000 feet in our area. (Flat-topped aster.) A flowering plant is shown on Pl. 30, 1.

(9)   **Pearly Everlasting**   *Anaphalis margaritacea* (L.) C. B. Clarke. In the pearly everlasting the heads are conspicuous not for their florets but for the white involucral bracts. The species is divided into a number of varieties. The very woolly plants of the lowlands belong to var. *intercedens* Hara. The material found above treeline is mostly var. *margaritacea*, which differs in having fewer leaves on the stem; these leaves are broader, blunter, and greener and less hairy on the upper surface. Some of the alpine material appears to be var. *subalpina* Gray which differs in being more dwarfed and in having the pubescence ash-colored rather than white. The species as a whole is found in eastern Asia and over much of North America south to North Carolina and Kansas. An inflorescence is shown on Pl. 29, 2.

(10)   **Mountain Cudweed**   *Gnaphalium supinum* L. This is the smallest composite to be found above timberline and it is also the most inconspicuous. The plants are less than 4 inches tall; the leaves are mostly basal with a silky rather than woolly pubescence; the heads are few, small, and have brown rather than white involucral bracts. The famous edelweiss of the Alps belongs to the same tribe of composites as this and the previous species. The species is a circumpolar arctic-alpine plant. On this continent it occurs on Mt. Washington, Katahdin, the mountains of Gaspé and north to Labrador and Greenland. A plant is shown on Pl. 30, 3.

(11)   **Yarrow**   *Achillea borealis* Bong. The yarrow is probably a familiar lowland plant to most readers; this is *A. Millefolium* L., a species which has the stem nearly smooth to somewhat cobwebby. *A. lanulosa* Nutt. is very similar but has the stem heavily woolly. In both these species the involucral bracts are colorless to light brown. *A. borealis* Bong. differs from these other two by having dark brown to black margins on the involucral bracts and slightly fewer leaves on the stem. This group of species sorely needs further study. Most of the collections made above treeline appear to be *A. borealis* but some are apparently *A. Millefolium*. *A. Millefolium* is an Old World species which is a common weed in North America. *A. borealis* is a circumboreal species which occurs in North America from Labrador to Alaska and south to northern New England and the Rocky Mountains. An inflorescence is shown on Pl. 30, 4.

(12)   **Arnica**   *Arnica mollis* Hook. The arnica is the largest-flowered and most conspicuous of the yellow-flowered composites above treeline, the heads often being more than two inches broad. The plants are usually in fine bloom on the headwalls of the ravines about the first of August. Two varieties are recognized. In var. *mollis* all but the lowest pair of leaves are rounded at the base and sessile. In var. *petiolaris* Fern. all but the upper pair of leaves are narrowed at the base to a slender petiole and the heads are somewhat smaller. Var. *mollis* is found from the Gaspé Peninsula to the mountains of Maine and New Hampshire and also from Alberta and British Columbia south to Colorado and California. Var. *petiolaris* occurs in Bonaventure Co., Quebec, and the White Mountains; with us it is much less common than var. *mollis*. Plants and an enlarged blossom are shown on Pl. 31, 1 and 2.

a. **Low Rattlesnake-root**
Prenanthes trifoliolata, var. *nana*

b. **Tall Rattlesnake-root**
Prenanthes altissima

c. **Boott's Rattlesnake-root**
Prenanthes Boottii

(13)   **Low Rattlesnake-root**   *Prenanthes trifoliolata* (Cass.) Fern., var. *nana* (Bigel.) Fern. The rattlesnake-roots differ from all the other composites growing above timberline in having the heads made up entirely of ray flowers. The leaves are very variable in shape in all three species. This and the next species often have the basal leaves deeply cleft into three lobes. In this species the involucre is made up of from six to eight conspicuous primary bracts and a number of much smaller secondary bracts. The heads are

135

nine- to twelve-flowered. The low rattlesnake-root grows from Labrador and Newfoundland to the mountains of New England and New York. Heads are shown on Pl. 31, 3; a plant on p. 135, a.

(14) **Tall Rattlesnake-root** *Prenanthes altissima* L. The tall rattlesnake-root is a wide-ranging species of the lowlands, which occasionally wanders above treeline. It is taller than the previous species and its leaf shape is very variable. The heads are greenish rather than blackish and there are only five primary bracts and five or six flowers. The species occurs from Quebec to Manitoba and south to Georgia. Heads are shown on Pl. 31, 4; a plant on p. 135, b.

(15) **Boott's Rattlesnake-root** *Prenanthes Boottii* (DC.) Gray. Boott's rattlesnake-root is the most dwarfed of the three species. The leaves are never cleft and at least some of the lowest leaves are heart-shaped. The heads are large, with ten to fifteen primary bracts and ten to eighteen flowers. The species is named for John Wright Boott, who visited the White Mountains in 1816 and 1829. The species is restricted to the mountains of northern New England and New York. A head is shown on Pl. 28, 6; a plant on p. 135, c.

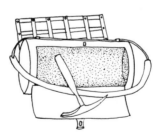

Plant press, vasculum and pick

GLOSSARY

Achene: a small, dry, one-seeded fruit that does not open at maturity.

Ament: a catkin; a soft, usually scaly, spike of small, apetalous, ordinarily unisexual flowers; usually falling as a unit.

Awn: a bristle-like appendage. See drawing, p. 39.

Axil: the angle between the upper side of the leaf and the stem.

Bidentate: two-toothed.

Bloom: a whitish powdery covering of a surface; what you polish off an apple.

Bract: a modified and reduced leaf-like structure.

Capsule: a dry fruit, derived from a compound pistil, which at maturity opens and allows the seeds to escape.

Ciliate: marginally fringed with hairs.

Cleistogamous: fertilized in the bud, without the opening of the flower.

Compound: composed of a number of similar parts, opposite of simple.

Culm: the stem of a grass or sedge.

Drupe: a fleshy fruit containing one stone or occasionally several.

Entire: without toothing or division of any kind.

Family: a unit of classification above a genus and below an order; composed of one or more genera.

Floret: a small flower; the flower of a grass plus the immediately enclosing bracts, the lemma and palea. See drawing, p. 29.

Frond: the leaf-blade of a fern.

Genus: a group of closely related species clearly marked off from other groups.

Glabrous: not hairy.

Globose: spherical or almost spherical.

Glume: a chaff-like bract; one of the empty bracts at the base of a grass spikelet. See drawing, p. 29.

Glutinous: sticky.

Herb: a plant with no woody tissue above ground level.
Herbaceous: not woody.

Indusium: the membranous covering of the sorus or fruit dot of a fern.
Involucre: a series of bracts surrounding a flower cluster or head. See drawing, p. 129.

Keel: the ridge along the outside of a fold.

Lemma: the lower of the two bracts enclosing the flower of a grass. See drawing, p. 29.
Ligule: a flat membranous scale produced at the point of joining of the sheath and blade of a grass leaf.

Monocotyledon: a flowering plant with one seed-leaf or cotyledon.

Obovate: egg-shaped with the attached end the narrower.
Ovate: egg-shaped with the attached end the broader.

Palea: the upper of the two bracts enclosing the flower of a grass. See drawing, p. 29.
Palmate: radiately lobed or divided; hand-like.
Panicle: a loose irregularly compound inflorescence with pedicellate flowers.
Papillose: bearing small nipple-like projections.
Pappus: the specialized calyx of members of the Composite Family; usually consisting of a ring of bristles or scales attached to the summit of the achene.
Pedicel: the stem of a single flower.
Peduncle: a primary flower stalk, supporting either a cluster or a single flower.
Perfect: applied to a flower having both functional pistils and functional stamens.
Perianth: collective term applied to the parts of the calyx and corolla, whatever their form. See drawing, p. 13.
Perigynium: the inflated sac which encloses the achene in *Carex*.
Petiole: the stalk of a leaf.
Pilose: soft hairy.
Pinna: a primary leaflet of a pinnately compound leaf.
Pinnate: having lobes or leaflets arising from either side of a common axis; feather-like.
Pinnule: a leaflet of a compound pinna.

Rhizome: an underground stem.

Rootstock: same as rhizome; an underground stem, not a root.

Samara: a dry winged fruit.

Saprophyte: an organism that obtains its food from nonliving organic matter.

Scurfy: with bran-like particles on surface.

Sessile: without a stalk.

Sheath: the base of a leaf that wraps around the stem, as in the grasses.

Simple: composed of a single unit, opposite of compound.

Sinus: a cleft or recess between two lobes.

Species: a population of individuals similar enough to have come from the same parents. May be either singular or plural.

Spike: an elongated inflorescence composed of essentially sessile flowers.

Spikelet: the unit of the inflorescence of a grass, consisting of two glumes and one or more florets. See drawing, p. 29.

Sporangium: a spore-case in which spores are formed.

Sporophyll: a sporangium-bearing leaf or bract.

Stipe: the leaf-stalk of a fern frond.

Stipule: an appendage on either side of the base of the leaf of some plants.

Stool: a compact clump of erect stems, as in some sedges.

Strobilus: a cone-like reproductive structure composed of a number of sporophylls.

Suborbicular: almost circular.

Ternate: three-parted.

Umbel: an inflorescence in which the flower stalks arise from the same point, like the ribs of an umbrella.

Vascular: Furnished with vessels or ducts.

Whorl: three or more leaves or scales arranged in a circle around the stem.

INDEX

141

143

144

KEY TO COMMON PLANTS FOUND IN THE FALL ABOVE TREELINE ON MOUNT WASHINGTON

This key is designed for use in the fall when few, if any, of the alpine plants are flowering, and for this reason is based on leaf characteristics alone. There are some dangers in relying on leaf features in that they show more "environmental plasticity" (sensitivity to environmental modifications) than do floral features. However, experience with this key has shown that the differences between the leaves of the different plants are sufficiently great so that identification is a relatively simple process.

There are two major groups of flowering plants, the Monocotyledons and the Dicotyledons. The Monocotyledons include such plants as the grasses, the sedges and a number of herbaceous plants, all having the characteristic of parallel veins in their leaves. In addition, the floral parts are in threes or multiples thereof. The Dicotyledons are flowering plants which have net-veined leaves and the floral parts are generally in fours or fives or multiples of these. They may be herbaceous or woody.

There are two sections to this key. Section A includes the herbaceous, that is, non-woody Monocotyledons and Dicotyledons, whereas Section B deals with the shrubs, that is, the woody-stemmed, perennial Dicotyledons.

No attempt has been made to subdivide the grasses, rushes and sedges further. Frequently in the fall these plants still retain their seed heads and identification can be made with the use of the keys located elsewhere in this book.

SECTION A. HERBACEOUS (NON-WOODY) PLANTS

1a Leaves with principal veins parallel, stems not woody.
.....MONOCOTYLEDON   2.

1b Leaves net-veined, stems woody or herbaceous.
.....DICOTYLEDON   6.
(FOR SHRUBS GO TO SECTION B)

2a Stems round or flat, hollow; Leaves 2-ranked, grass-like, lower sheathing split....GRASSES OR RUSHES

2b Stems not as above... 3.

3a Stems often triangular, leaves 3-ranked, the sheaths not split. Leaves grass-like.............................SEDGES

3b Leaves not grass-like — thicker, different shape, etc. ... 4.

4a Leaves 1″-3″ long, oval or heart-shaped, 1 or 2 leaves present, leaf-stalks 1″-4″ long.

Canada Mayflower. *Maianthemum canadense* (p. 68)

4b Leaves longer than 3″.. 5.

5a Leaves 6″-12″ long. Plant conspicuous by ht. 1-3 ft. Leaves strongly veined.

Indian Poke. *Veratrum viride* (p. 67)

5b Leaves 2″ to 5″, oval, oblong, not strongly veined.

Clintonia. *Clintonia borealis* (p. 68)

6a Leaves opposite.. 7.
6b Leaves basal.. 8.
6c Leaves alternate... 9.

7a Leaves narrow, linear, upper lvs. distant, lower lvs. matted. Ht. 2″-4″.

Mountain Sandwort. *Arenaria groenlandica* (p. 83)

7b Leaves oval, rounded at base and tip. Plant hairy.

Alpine Speedwell. *Veronica alpina* var. *unalaschensis*

(p. 122)

8a Leaf blade divided into 3 dark green leaflets, long leaf-stalk. Rootstock bright yellow.

Goldthread. *Coptis groenlandica* (p. 86)

8b Leaves thin, broadly oval or kidney-shaped with wavy margins, 1″-1½″ wide.

Northern Marsh Violet. *Viola palustris* (p. 106)

9a Leaf blade entire... 11.
9b Leaf blade divided into leaflets.............................. 10.

10a Leaf blade clearly divided into 3 nearly-equal leaflets. Tip of each leaflet 3-toothed.

Three-toothed Cinquefoil. *Potentilla tridentata* (p. 96)

10b Leaf blade divided into one large leaflet and two small leaflets. Small leaflets below large one. Large one rounded, irregularly toothed.

Mountain Avens. *Geum Peckii* (p. 98)

11a Leaves rounded or kidney-shaped.............................. 12.
11b Leaves oval with a pointed tip, lanceolate, or oblong.. 13.

12a Leaf irregularly toothed.

Mountain Avens. *Geum Peckii* (p. 98)

12b Leaf not toothed, mainly kidney-shaped, hairless, elongated leaf stalks.

Mountain Sorrel. *Oxyria digyna* (p. 81)

13a Leaves oval with pointed tip — rounded at base, small — a few rounded teeth, green and shiny.

Alpine Cress. *Cardamine bellidifolia* (p. 89)

13b Leaves not as above....................................... 14.

14a Basal leaves heart-shaped, upper leaves lanceolate. Upper leaves may lack a stalk.
> **Boott's Rattlesnake-root.** *Prenanthes Boottii* (p. 136)

14b Basal leaves lanceolate, pointed a⁺ apex, rounded at base. Stem leaves narrow, linear, grasslike.
> **Alpine Bistort.** *Polygonum viviparum* (p. 82)

SECTION B. WOODY PERENNIAL SHRUBS

1a Leaves opposite.. 2.

1b Leaves alternate... 4.

1c Leaves densely crowded on stem.................................... 18.

2a Leaves crowded and small, midrib apparently absent, leaves closely adpressed to stem, giving a 4-sided appearance, blunt tipped, 1/16″-3/16″ long.
> **Moss Plant.** *Cassiope hypnoides* (p. 116)

2b Leaves not crowded... 3.

3a Leaves without a stalk or nearly so; whitened beneath. Twigs 2-edged. Leaf margins rolled.
> **Pale Laurel.** *Kalmia polifolia* (p. 115)

3b Leaves with a stalk, midrib very prominent on lower surface. Leaf margins rolled, leaves 1/8″-3/8″ long. Plants form small mats 1/4″ high.
> **Alpine Azalea.** *Loiseleuria procumbens* (p. 114)

4a Leaves with toothed margins — rounded or pointed teeth.. 5.

4b Leaf margins not toothed... 7.

5a Leaves rounded, thin, rarely exceeding 1/2″ diam. Teeth wavy. Bright green on both sides. Bark bitter. Leaves not aromatic. Forms dense mats 1/2″-1″ in height. **Dwarf Willow.** *Salix Herbacea* (p. 73)

5b Leaves not as above... 6.

6a Leaves nearly without a stalk, green, shiny on both sides. Teeth blunt. Leaves egg-shaped, blunt end at tip, 1/2″-1⅝″ long. Plant forms tufts 2″-4″ in height.
> **Dwarf Bilberry.** *Vaccinium cespitosum* (p. 118)

6b Leaves stalked, teeth rounded, veins prominent — 1/4″-1″ long, deep green on upper surface — pale beneath. Ht. 1″-3″. Twigs brown — bark bitter.
> **Bearberry Willow.** *Salix Uva-ursi* (p. 74)

7a Leaves without a stalk or nearly so................................ 8.

7b Leaves stalked.. 9.

8a Leaves densely crowded, without a stalk, purplish-green. Plants forming conspicuous low rounded mats or cushions. **Diapensia.** *Diapensia lapponica* (p. 120)

8b Leaves nearly without a stalk, not densely crowded, narrow at base, rounded at tip, thick, smooth; dull, pale or glaucous beneath. 3/16"-7/8" long.

Bog Bilberry. *Vaccinium uliginosum* (p. 118)

9a Leaves or other plant parts covered with hairs, scales or woolly covering.. 10.

9b Leaves or other plant parts not as above........................ 13.

10a Leaves evergreen, leathery, underside coating of dense brown woolly hairs. Leaf margins rolled; leaves 1/2"-2" long, fragrant when crushed. Ht. 4"-12". Plant erect. **Labrador Tea.** *Ledum groenlandicum* (p. 113)

10b Leaves not as above...................................... 11.

11a Whole plant covered with rusty scales and dots. Plant prostrate. Lvs. narrow, leathery, 1/4"-3/4". Ht. rarely exceeds 1".

Lapland Rosebay. *Rhododendron lapponicum* (p. 114)

11b Plant without rusty scales.................................. 12.

12a Leaves evergreen, narrow, underside covered with white hairs: Margins rolled, petiole short, lvs. 1"-1½" long. **Bog-Rosemary.** *Andromeda glaucophylla* (p. 115)

12b Leaves deciduous, dark green above, pale and downy below. Petiole short, lvs. oval-oblong.

Rhodora. *Rhododendron canadense* (p. 114)

13a Leaves thick, evergreen.................................. 14.

13b Leaves thin, deciduous.................................. 15.

14a Leaves crowded, oval shape, shiny above, paler and with black dots below. Lvs. 1/4"-3/4", not pointed. Ht. 1"-2" (4" in protected areas).

Mountain Cranberry. *Vaccinium Vitis-Idaea* (p. 119)

14b Leaves pointed, dark green above, whitish below. Margins rolled. Lvs. 3/8" long. Plant trailing or erect.

Wren's Egg Cranberry. *Vaccinium Oxycoccos* (p. 119)

15a Twigs dark purple-green or dark green and shiny....... 16.

15b Twigs not as above...................................... 17.

16a Leaves 1"-3" long. Twigs dark purple-green. Plant height 1-4 ft. Bark bitter tasting. (May have minute teeth) **Tea-leaved Willow.** *Salix planifolia* (p. 76)

16b Twigs dark green, shiny. Lvs. bright green above, silver below. 3/4"-2.5" in length. Bark bitter. Ht. 1-4 ft.

Silver Willow. *Salix argyrocarpa* (p. 74)

Iceland Lichen, x 1
Cetraria islandica
See page 6

Peat Moss, x 1
Sphagnum sp.
See page 8

2. Snow Lichen, x ⅝
Cetraria nivalis
See page 7

4. Peat Moss, x ½
Sphagnum sp.
See page 8

17a Leaves pointed, green both sides; branches green and warty. Stems very branched. Lvs. 1/4″-1⅛″ long. Ht. 2″-4″.

Low Sweet Blueberry. *Vaccinium angustifolium* (p. 118)

17b Leaves rounded at tips, narrow towards petiole. Veins strongly developed, giving blade a wrinkled appearance.

Alpine Bearberry. *Arctostaphylos alpina* (p. 116)

18a Leaves very densely crowded on stem, sessile, closely adpressed to stem — appears 4-sided — looks like a moss. Leaves apparently veinless, blunt-tipped, 1/16″-3/16″ long. Ht. 1″-5″.

Moss Plant. *Cassiope hypnoides* (p. 116)

18b Leaves not as above.. 19.

19a Leaves needle-like, sharp tipped, 1/8″-1/4″ long, not arranged in 4 rows. Ht. 2″-3″.

Black Crowberry. *Empetrum nigrum* (p. 101)

19b Leaves are like blunt, flat needles 3/16″-3/8″ long. Ht. 4″-6″. Older bark is flaky.

Mountain Heath. *Phyllodoce caerulea* (p. 115)

CHRISTINE D. JOHNSON

References

BLISS, L. C.; *Alpine Zone of the Presidential Range* (pamphlet).

BRITTON, N. L. AND BROWN, L.; *An Illustrated Flora of the Northern United States and Canada,* New York, N.Y.: Dover Publications, 1970, three volumes.

1. British Soldiers, x ⅔
   Cladonia cristatella
   See page 6

2. Reinde
   Cladoni
   See pag

3. Alpine Reindeer Lichen, x 1
   Cladonia alpestris
   See page 6

4. Ring Li
   Parmeli
   See page

PLATE 3

1. Stud Lichen, x ⅔
   Ochrolechia frigida
   See page 4

2. Rock Tripe, x ⅔
   Umbilicaria hyperborea
   See page 4

3. Map Lichen, x ½
   Rhizocarpon geographicum
   See page 3

4. Worm Lichen, x ¾
   Thamnolia vermicularis
   See page 7

5. Mane Lichen, x ⅓
   Alectoria ochroleuca
   See page 7

6. Hair-cap Moss, x ⅔
   Polytrichum juniperinum, var. *alpestre*
   See page 8

PLATE 4

1. Fir Clubmoss, x 1
   Lycopodium Selago
   See page 19

2. Shining Clubmoss, x ½
   Lycopodium lucidulum
   See page 19

3. Bristly Clubmoss, x 1
   Lycopodium annotinum
   See page 19

4. Groundpine, x ⅓
   Lycopodium obscurum, var. *dendroideum*
   See page 20

PLATE 5

1. Running Clubmoss, x ¼
   Lycopodium clavatum
   See page 19
2. Rusty Woodsia, x ¼
   Woodsia ilvensis
   See page 22
3. Running Pine, x ¼
   Lycopodium complanatum, var. *flabelliforme*
   See page 20
4. Common Polypody, x ¼
   Polypodium virginianum
   See page 26
5. Lady Fern, x ⅛
   Athyrium Filix-femina
   See page 25
6. Black Spruce, x ⅛
   Picea mariana
   See page 28

PLATE 6

1. Interrupted Fern, x $\frac{1}{10}$
   Osmunda Claytoniana
   See page 21

2. Spinulose Wood Fern, x $\frac{1}{8}$
   Dryopteris spinulosa
   See page 24

3. Bracken, x $\frac{1}{5}$
   Pteridium aquilinum, var. *latiusculum*
   See page 25

4. Balsam Fir, x $\frac{2}{3}$
   Abies balsamea
   See page 27

PLATE 7

1. Juniper, x 1
   Juniperus communis
   See page 28

2. Larch, x ½
   Larix laricina
   See page 28

3. Deer's Hair, x ⅓
   Scirpus cespitosus, var. *callosus*
   See page 48

4. Hare's Tail, x 2
   Eriophorum spissum
   See page 48

PLATE 8

1. Highland Rush, x ½
   Juncus trifidus
   See page 62

2. Short-tailed Rush, x ½
   Juncus brevicaudatus
   See page 64

3. Small-flowered Woodrush, x ½
   Luzula parviflora, var. *melanocarpa*
   See page 64

4. Indian Poke, x ¼
   Veratrum viride
   See page 67

PLATE 9

1. Canada Mayflower, x 2
   Maianthemum canadense
   See page 68

2. Three-leaved False Solomon's-seal, x ½
   Smilacina trifolia
   See page 68

3. Clintonia, x 1
   Clintonia borealis
   See page 68

4. Painted Trillium, x 1
   Trillium undulatum
   See page 70

PLATE 10

1. Sessile-leaved Twisted-stalk, x ½
   Streptopus roseus
   See page 70

2. Clasping-leaved Twisted-stalk, x ½
   Streptopus amplexifolius, var. *americanus*
   See page 69

3. Tall Leafy White Orchid, x 1
   Habenaria dilatata
   See page 71

4. Heart-leaved Twayblade, x ⅓
   Listera cordata
   See page 72

PLATE 11

1. Dwarf Willow, x ¾
   Salix herbacea
   See page 73

2. False Spikenard, x ¼
   Smilacina racemosa
   See page 68

3. Bearberry Willow, female plant, x ¾
   Salix Uva-ursi
   See page 74

4. Bearberry Willow, male plant, x ¾
   Salix Uva-ursi
   See page 74

5. Whitlow-wort, x 1
   Paronychia argyrocoma, var. *albimontana*
   See page 83

6. Spring Beauty, x 1
   Claytonia caroliniana
   See page 82

PLATE 12

1. Mountain Sorrel, x 1
   Oxyria digyna
   See page 81

2. Alpine Bistort, x 2
   Polygonum viviparum
   See page 82

3. Mountain alder, x $\frac{1}{4}$
   Alnus crispa
   See page 80

4. Dwarf Birch, x 1
   Betula glandulosa
   See page 80

PLATE 13

1. Mountain Sandwort, x 1
   Arenaria groenlandica
   See page 83

2. Sundew, x 1
   Drosera rotundifolia
   See page 89

3. Goldthread, x 1½
   Coptis groenlandica
   See page 86

4. Alpine Brook Saxifrage, x 2
   Saxifraga rivularis
   See page 90

PLATE 14

1. Tall Meadow Rue, x 2
   Thalictrum polygamum
   See page 86

2. Star-like Saxifrage, var. *comosa*, x ½
   Saxifraga stellaris
   See page 90

3. Alpine Cress, x 1
   Cardamine bellidifolia
   See page 89

4. Northern Stitchwort, x 1
   Stellaria calycantha
   See page 85

5. Dwarf Cinquefoil, x 1½
   Potentilla Robbinsiana
   See page 98

6. Moss Campion, x 2
   Silene acaulis
   See page 85

PLATE 15

1. Skunk Currant, x ½
   Ribes glandulosum
   See page 92

2. Swamp Black Currant, x 1
   Ribes lacustre
   See page 92

3. Northern Meadowsweet, x 1
   Spirea latifolia, var. *septentrionalis*
   See page 94

4. American Mountain Ash, x ¼
   Pyrus americana
   See page 95

PLATE 16

1. Juneberry, x ¼
   Amelanchier Bartramiana
   See page 95

3. Sibbaldia, x 1
   Sibbaldia procumbens
   See page 96

2. Wild Strawberry, x 1
   Fragaria virginiana, var. *terra-novae*
   See page 96

4. Dwarf Raspberry, x 1
   Rubus pubescens
   See page 99

PLATE 17

1. Three-toothed Cinquefoil, x 3
   Potentilla tridentata
   See page 96
2. Purple Avens, x 1⅓
   Geum rivale
   See page 98
3. Three-toothed Cinquefoil, x 1
   Potentilla tridentata
   See page 96
4. Mountain Avens, x 1
   Geum Peckii
   See page 98
5. Baked-apple Berry, x 1
   Rubus Chamaemorus
   See page 98
6. Common Wood Sorrel, x ½
   Oxalis montana
   See page 100

PLATE 18

1. Fireweed, x ½
   Epilobium angustifolium
   See page 107

2. Hornemann's Willow-herb, x 2
   Epilobium Hornemanni
   See page 107

3. Marsh Willow-herb, x 1½
   Epilobium palustre
   See page 107

4. Wild Sarsaparilla, x ⅙
   Aralia nudicaulis
   See page 109

PLATE 19

1. Northern Marsh Violet, x 2
   Viola palustris
   See page 106

2. Wild White Violet, x 2
   Viola pallens
   See page 106

3. Rhodora, x ¼
   Rhododendron canadense
   See page 114

4. B nchberry, x 1
   Cornus canadensis
   See page 111

5. Labrador Tea, x ¾
   Ledum groenlandicum
   See page 113

6. Bunchberry, x ½
   Cornus canadensis
   See page 111

PLATE 20

1. Black Crowberry, x 2
   Empetrum nigrum
   See page 101

2. Black Crowberry, x 1
   Empetrum nigrum
   See page 101

3. Indian Pipe, x $\frac{3}{4}$
   Monotropa uniflora
   See page 111

4. Alpine Azalea, x 2
   Loiseleuria procumbens
   See page 114

PLATE 21

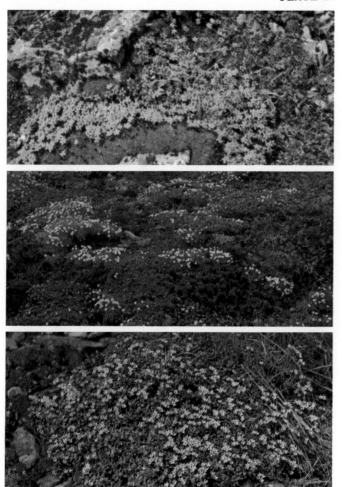

1. Moss Campion
   Silene acaulis
   See page 85

2. Lapland Rosebay,
   Diapensia and Alpine Azalea
   See pages 114 and 120

3. Alpine Azalea
   Loiseleuria procumbens
   See page 114

PLATE 22

1. Lapland Rosebay, x ½
   Rhododendron lapponicum
   See page 114

2. Moss Plant, x ⅓
   Cassiope hypnoides
   See page 116

3. Lapland Rosebay, x 2
   Rhododendron lapponicum
   See page 114

4. Mountain Heath, x 1
   Phyllodoce caerulea
   See page 115

PLATE 23

1. Pale Laurel, x 1
   Kalmia polifolia
   See page 115

2. Sheep Laurel, x 1
   Kalmia angustifolia
   See page 115

3. Low Sweet Blueberry, x $\frac{1}{3}$
   Vaccinium angustifolium
   See page 116

4. Moss Plant, x $1\frac{1}{2}$
   Cassiope hypnoides
   See page 116

5. Alpine Bearberry, x $\frac{3}{4}$
   Arctostaphylos alpina
   See page 116

6. Creeping Snowberry, x 1
   Gaultheria hispidula
   See page 116

PLATE 24

1. Bog Bilberry, x ½
   Vaccinium uliginosum, var. *alpinum*
   See page 118
3. Mountain Cranberry, x 1
   Vaccinium Vitis-Idaea, var. *minus*
   See page 119
5. Wren's Egg Cranberry, x 2
   Vaccinium Oxycoccos
   See page 119

2. Bog Bilberry, x 2
   Vaccinium uliginosum, var. *alpinum*
   See page 118
4. Mountain Cranberry, x 2
   Vaccinium Vitis-Idaea, var. *minus*
   See page 119
6. Wren's Egg Cranberry, x 1
   Vaccinium Oxycoccos
   See page 119

PLATE 25

1. Velvet-leaf Blueberry, x ½
   Vaccinium myrtilloides
   See page 118

2. Alpine Speedwell, x 3
   Veronica alpina, var. *unalaschcensis*
   See page 122

3. Pale Painted Cup, x 1
   Castilleja septentrionalis
   See page 122

4. Self-heal, x 1½
   Prunella vulgaris, var. *lanceolata*
   See page 121

PLATE 26

1. Star Flower, x 3
   Trientalis borealis
   See page 120

2. Star Flower, x ¾
   Trientalis borealis
   See page 120

3. Diapensia, x 1
   Diapensia lapponica
   See page 120

4. Alpine Bluet, x 1
   Houstonia caerulea, var. *Faxonorum*
   See page 125

5. Closed Gentian, x ½
   Gentiana linearis
   See page 120

6. Twinflower, x 2
   Linnaea borealis, var. *americana*
   See page 126

PLATE 27

1. Cow-wheat, x 1½
   Melampyrum lineare, var. *lineare*
   See page 123

2. Yellow Rattle, x 1½
   Rhinanthus borealis
   See page 124

3. Mountain Fly Honeysuckle, x ⅔
   Lonicera villosa
   See page 126

4. Squashberry, x ½
   Viburnum edule
   See page 128

PLATE 28

1. Bluebell, x ½
   Campanula rotundifolia
   See page 128

2. Eyebright, x 1
   Euphrasia Williamsii
   See page 124

3. Bluebell, x 2
   Campanula rotundifolia
   See page 128

4. Hobblebush, x $\frac{1}{10}$
   Viburnum alnifolium
   See page 126

5. Rough-bracted Aster, x 1
   Aster radula
   See page 132

6. Boott's Rattlesnake-root, x 1½
   Prenanthes Boottii
   See page 136

PLATE 29

1. Eyebright, x 3
   Euphrasia Williamsii
   See page 124

2. Pearly Everlasting, x 1
   Anaphalis margaritacea
   See page 134

3. Large-leaved Goldenrod, x ½
   Solidago macrophylla, var. *thrysoidea*
   See page 131

4. Alpine Goldenrod, x 1
   Solidago Cutleri
   See page 131

PLATE 30

1. Umbellate Aster, x ½
   Aster umbellatus
   See page 133

2. Sharp-leaved Wood Aster, x ½
   Aster acuminatus
   See page 133

3. Mountain Cudweed, x ½
   Gnaphalium supinum
   See page 134

4. Yarrow, x 1
   Achillea borealis
   See page 134

PLATE 31

1. Arnica, x $\frac{1}{8}$
   Arnica mollis
   See page 135

2. Arnica, x $1\frac{1}{2}$
   Arnica mollis
   See page 135

3. Low Rattlesnake-root, x 1
   Prenanthes trifoliolata, var. *nana*
   See page 135

4. Tall Rattlesnake-root, x 1
   Prenanthes altissima
   See page 136

PLATE 32

1. Monroe Flats
   Mt. Washington

2. Pamola and Chimney Peak
   Katahdin

3. The Great Gulf
   White Mountains

4. Edmands Col
   White Mountains

5. The Alpine Garden
   Mt. Washington

6. Autumn on Mt. Bigelow
   Maine